The Drive

Megan Maher

ISBN 979-8-89428-022-6 (paperback)
ISBN 979-8-89526-004-3 (hardcover)
ISBN 979-8-89428-023-3 (digital)

Christian Faith Publishing
832 Park Avenue
Meadville, PA 16335
www.christianfaithpublishing.com

Printed in the United States of America

For peace

Introduction

Can you recover from loss? Grief? Trauma? Anxiety? Depression? Like, actually fully recover from it. What happens when the therapy doesn't help anymore? Or you build a tolerance to the medications? Do you ever REALLY move past it? Can you get the image of someone you love lying in a casket out of your brain? Or the image of the morbid makeup caked on their face by the coroner? A coroner you've never even seen or met before. Can you get the musty smell of your loved one's last breath out of your nostrils? Can you get the screaming, the crying, and the mourning out of your ears? Can you move past the pain of watching a Persian-American family lose their son to a terminal brain tumor at the age of twenty-six? Can you forget the brown rusted color of the casket that is now the home to his body? Do you ever forget watching his mourning brother struggle to give an impossible eulogy for a death that is just so painfully unfair, so painfully tragic, so painfully unimaginable? Do you forget the blackness? The blackness that engulfs your vision as you stare into the crowd while reading your boyfriend's eulogy? Can you honestly move past this level of grief? A level of grief you sincerely didn't know existed. How do you move past watching your boyfriend be lowered into the cold, hard ground in a glossy brown casket at the age of twenty-six? How do you move forward after experiencing this level of grief and pain?

What do you do when you cannot sleep at night because you cannot get these images out of your head? How do you cope when all you can hear are the shrieks and screams of his mourning family members ringing in your ears? How do you get the taste of incense out of your mouth? How do you get the flashing lights and sirens from ambulances out of your head? How do you get the smell of death out of your nose? How do you move forward without the trauma fully engulfing you?

How do you actually recover from this?

This is not a sad story. I am not writing this to sadden or discourage you. I am not writing this story to give you another hopeless example of how God can be so unfair, so misunderstood, so seemingly calculated, so punishing, and so angry. Or as another hopeless example of how the world can be so evil, dark, lonely, and senseless. I am purposely starting this story with Arash's burial. I am purposely starting with what I thought was the end of my love story with Arash Perri but have since come to realize this ending was really just a continuation of a love that has always been present. A love that was always meant to be exactly what it was. A love that is strong, unchanging, unmoving, and unfaltering in the midst of a truly horrible diagnosis.

A terminal, cancerous, rapidly metastasizing brain tumor.

Arash was diagnosed with anaplastic astrocytoma on Friday, August 13th, 2021.

The World Health Organization (WHO) reclassified anaplastic astrocytoma as a "grade 3 astrocytoma" in 2021.

A grade 3 astrocytoma is a fast-growing brain tumor made up of astrocyte cells. Astrocytes are star-shaped cells in your brain and spinal cord that support and protect neurons, or nerve cells. As a grade 3 tumor, this classification means that it grows faster and is more aggressive than grades 1 and 2. While less common, it can spread to neighboring brain tissue from where the tumor started growing. It's also known as malignant (cancerous) or high-grade astrocytoma. Worldwide, approximately 5 to 8 people out of every 100,000 receive a grade 3 or a grade 4 astrocytoma tumor (glioblastoma) diagnosis each year (Cleveland Clinic).

So approximately 0.5% of people will be diagnosed with this every year.

Typically, treatment for a grade 3 astrocytoma includes a combination of surgical removal of the tumor, radiation, and chemotherapy. Side effects of surgery include bleeding, infection, headaches, hydrocephalus (swelling of the brain), pain, and seizures. Side effects of radiation and chemotherapy may include bleeding or infection, constipation, diarrhea, fatigue, headaches, hair loss, nausea, vomiting, and reduced appetite (Cleveland Clinic).

Arash's prognosis was approximately 7 months. Arash passed away on Friday, June 19th, 2022. Father's Day and Juneteenth. Arash was my boyfriend. He was my best friend. He became part of my family. I became part of his family.

He was the love of my life.

Part 1

Grief

Chapter 1

The Burial and Funeral

When someone you love becomes a memory,
the memory becomes a treasure.

—Anonymous

I can still play Arash's burial in my mind like a scene out of a horror movie. Actually, this was worse than a horror movie. Because this was real. This actually happened. This was truly a traumatizing event. After Arash's funeral, I walked alongside my father and brother, Sean, as eight pallbearers carried Arash's casket and placed it into the back of the long black hearse. These pallbearers were Arash's best friends and cousins that I had grown to know very well over the previous four years. I can still smell the incense accompanying his casket. I can still see the tears welling up in the pallbearers' eyes. I can see these grown men trying to hold back tears as they carry their twenty-six-year-old friend's casket. I can see their black suits and their white gloves. I can hear the loud weeping of Arash's mom for the loss of her son. I can see Arash's dad trying to hold it together. He is about a minute away from total breakdown. I can see Arya, Arash's brother and best friend, with a look of pure numbness on his face. I can hear his family members shrieking in Farsi. I can see the sea of blackness and the funeral procession as they proceed to the cemetery down the road. I remember sitting in my father's car with my brother as we drove down the road to the cemetery. I remember looking out the window and seeing the cars stop for us as the funeral procession passes by. In that moment, I am extremely conscious that we are driving in our cars and they are not. They are still. The world stopped moving that day. But the sun was just starting to peek out from behind the clouds.

We arrive to the cemetery. The sea of blackness makes its way to Arash's gravesite in Algonquin, Illinois. The site is surrounded by Arash's family and some close friends. Weeping and shrieking fill your ears. The groundkeepers of the cemetery slowly crank the foundation that is holding Arash's casket, lowering it into the ground. The weeping and shrieking multiply.

Deacon Mike stands in front of Arash's casket and shares a prayer and words of hope for Arash in his new life. The sea of blackness slowly separates into individual people dressed in black who are taking turns tossing white roses on top of their dear son, their dear brother, their dear nephew, their dear cousin, their dear friend.

We say goodbye to Arash for the last time, and the sea of blackness again separates into individual people dressed in black who make their way to their cars still parked in the order of the funeral procession and proceed one by one out of the cemetery.

> You can see the pain in my laugh (yeah, yeah)
> Demons comin' back from the past (yeah, yeah)
> Feelin' like I'm 'bout to relapse (yeah, yeah)
> Voices in my head (yeah, yeah)
> All I can hear them say (yeah, yeah)
> Is, "Everyone wants me dead" (yeah, yeah)
> I'm already dead (yeah, yeah)
> I've been dead for years.
> (Juice WRLD, "Already Dead")

*****

I can also still play Arash's funeral in my mind like a scene out of a movie. It was June 25, 2022. It was a slightly chilly, rainy dreary summer morning. The clouds were covering the sky, and there wasn't a ray of sun shining through the unnaturally cloudy sky. The rain would come and go in waves. The rain felt extra heavy that morning. Starting as a drizzle and then building to a heavy downpour that seemed to flood the streets in an alternate world. The kind of rain that your car's windshield wipers can't keep up with. Within minutes, the heavy rain would stop and the cloudy sky would return. You could feel this rain in your bones. It was perfectly parallel to your mood.

My immediate family was getting ready for the funeral at my parents' house in Elmhurst, Illinois. My mother; my father; my sister, Shannon; my brothers Brendan and Sean; and Brendan's now-fiancée, Ali, were putting our rain gear on as we get ready to leave the house.

"Are we ready to go?" my dad asks.

"Yeah, let's go," my sister, Shannon, says.

My brother Brendan takes initiative and grabs his car keys, and we split up into two cars. My mother, Brendan, Shannon, and Ali file into one car. My father, Sean, and I file into my dad's car.

Everyone in the family was on edge. We were about to attend a funeral for a predominately Muslim family from Iran. Arash and his family had become family to us in the past four years, but nonetheless, we were an Irish Catholic family from the suburbs of Chicago and were facing the unfamiliarity of a Persian-American funeral. We were heartbroken, exhausted, and anxious. Very anxious.

Like all parts of that day, I vividly remember that drive to Arash's funeral. My dad sat in the driver's seat of his gray Acura. I was sitting in the passenger seat, and my brother Sean was sitting in the backseat. My dad's car was always extremely messy. I vividly remember having to move mountains of paperwork to the back seat to even sit down in the passenger seat. As I anticipate the unfamiliarity of the day, this moment of familiarity really warmed my heart.

I barely slept the night before. I mean, nothing in life prepares you for the death of the person you thought you were going to marry. You are in unchartered territory. You are simply trying to survive each day. I hadn't slept for months prior to this day, so I honestly didn't feel much different from any other day over the past few months.

As you can imagine, we didn't speak much on the way to the funeral. My dad had the radio on to a soft volume, and I remember clinging on to whatever Post Malone song was playing as the only type of distraction for what was about to come. My dad would occasionally ask me if I was okay, and I responded with a soft smile and a quiet "Yes." I don't remember the details of what my dad said to me that day in the car, but I remember the impact it had on me. I felt safe, I knew that whatever we were about to face, we would get through it because we had each other. I remember him saying, "This is probably going to be the worst day of your life," and somehow that didn't frighten me. It almost calmed me. Like we were saying goodbye to a horrible sickness who had taken who Arash was and quite literally buried him into the ground. He wouldn't be suffering anymore. And things had to get better. They certainly couldn't get worse.

It's hard not to sound insensitive when talking about this day. It was horrible and tragic for so many reasons but also relieving that we no longer had to watch the once-lively, vivacious young Arash Perri slowly deteriorate both mentally and physically from incurable brain cancer.

After what seemed like the longest car ride ever, we finally arrived at the funeral parlor, where my dad, Sean, and I slowly got out of the car. We truly did not know what to expect. We were walking into the unknown. I remember Sean gave me a hug, one I truly needed.

"You got this, Meg," Sean said.

In that moment, his sincere encouragement was what gave me the strength to walk through the doors.

*****

As I sit in Balboa Park in San Diego, California, writing this, I can hear Arash's infectious laugh bouncing off the walls of the San Diego Museum of Art. I can hear him laughing as he sits up above, chuckling at the nervousness of my white Irish Catholic family about to enter a Middle Eastern funeral. He's amusingly awaiting my lovely grandmother's well-intentioned but inevitably racially insensitive comments and awaiting the theatrics that is a Persian funeral.

My grandmother was one of Arash's favorite members of my family; the two would always spend time talking about the Chicago Bears and issues in the Middle East at our family Christmas parties. They are both in heaven having a Jim Beam on the rocks, discussing the prospects of the Bears as I write this.

*****

I can still feel the strength of the hug Mrs. Perri gave me when I entered the funeral parlor. I remember that I could feel her heart breaking as her body could no longer hold the weight of this grief. It had been an excruciatingly difficult past few months, and the amount of time we had all spent together was infinite. We had cried together, laughed together, mourned together; our families truly became one over the previous few weeks. Mrs. Perri was a stunning woman. She had beautiful brown eyes and was always dressed in bright colors, with bright makeup, and was always wearing jewelry—rings, bracelets, necklaces, you name it. To see her in all black, with eyeliner dripping down her face, was truly saddening. Truly not her. Truly her in an alternate form of herself.

Arya, Arash's younger brother, had so many similarities to Arash it was almost uncanny. He looked just like him. He, too, had his gorgeous, striking brown eyes, his dark hair, and the confidence that would make anyone fall in love with him. Arya had become like a brother to me in the last few months of Arash's life. He truly was grieving the loss of not only his brother but also his absolute best friend, his role model, his guy. Arya had stepped up in ways that are truly unimaginable. He took on responsibilities of making unimaginable decisions for his brother. To this day, I do not know how Arya was able to handle everything he was going through with such strength, poise, and love. He was truly a hero during this dark time, and I know Arash was forever grateful for everything he did for him.

*****

Sometimes, when the pain, trauma, and horror haunt me in the darkness of night, my vision is filled with the image of Arash's body lying in that casket. All I can see is my twenty-six-year-old boyfriend lying in a casket that was never meant to be his. Never meant to happen so soon. Not like this. Not so traumatically, not so quickly, not so painfully. I can see his thin face and the unnatural look of the foundation on his face lying in that casket as his mom literally drops to the floor in pain mourning for her son who was taken from this world way too soon, way too violently, and way too traumatically. I can still see the tears in his dad's eyes welling up as he tries to hold his emotions. I can still see the look of numbness on his family's face as they search for the words to say as they pass through the funeral line. I can see the tears in his countless friends' eyes as they search for meaning in why this happened as it did. I can feel the hugs from people who truly were at a loss for words and could only express how sorry they were with the strength of their hug because there really are no words to describe the depth of this grief. The depth of grief from a family who traveled from the war-stricken, constantly mourning Iran to America for a better life and were about to bury their first son. That sort of trauma, trauma that comes from generations of people traveling to America for a better life, it doesn't go away. It stays with you forever, but you find ways to cope with it, you find meaning in life past it. You learn from it. You grow from it. You hug your loved ones harder. You begin to cherish each day. You fall in love with where you are, who you're with, and what you're doing. No matter what that is. Because that trauma lives within you. It lives within all of us. The trauma is that internal war that's been raging inside us for as long as time.

Because to truly love, you have to lose. There's just no other way to it. There's no way around it. There's no easy escape from what is inevitable. This trauma, this pain that we inevitably have to face head-on is what allows us to weather life's most challenging storms, and it's what teaches us how to transform.

Arash knew this at an extremely young age. It's why I fell in love with him. A love made for the movies but fueled by the realness of pain, the realness of suffering, the realness of war, the realness of disease. A love not possible to live on in this life, but love that makes you find what you're searching for in the next life.

*****

Numbness.

Numbness is deafening. I think the numbness that comes with grief is the most extreme. With this numbness, you can actually see yourself looking at your life from an outsider's perspective. It's as if you stepped out of your own body and are watching this movie scene from another person's body. This numbness is the definition of disconnection. You are disconnected from your loved one lying in the casket. You are disconnected from the other people around you. You are disconnected from yourself. The numbness with grief feels like you can actually feel the particles in your body changing. You can feel your senses changing. The life that you had known prior to grief is gone, and now your senses have to reset themselves and adjust to this new norm. You can feel your emotions changing. Your happiness will never quite reach the same level as before. Your sadness will now reach record levels. Your body changes. Your brain chemistry changes. Everything changes.

When Arash was diagnosed with a terminal brain tumor, it felt like the world stopped moving. Like you were fast-forwarded to driving in the funeral procession and when you looked out the windows you could see the rest of the world standing still. Like everything you thought was true was, in fact, not true. Like everything you thought you could depend on, you cannot depend on. Like all the plans you thought you had for the future, God just took a judge's gavel and smashed those plans to smithereens. Like you were being robbed of the good in the world and it was being replaced with evil. Like you are swimming to the top of the ocean but can't quite get that breath. I became conscious of how different the grief was when Arash was first diagnosed with cancer and the grief that I was feeling in that moment looking at him in the casket. I became aware of the difference in the grief of the journey and the grief of the ultimate destination.

Funeral lines are weird. It's like you're standing there grieving, and one moment you're giving a hug to someone you've never met before, and within seconds you're giving a hug to someone you've known your whole life, and within seconds you're having an extremely awkward conversation with someone you barely know. When you're standing in the funeral line, you're so completely numb at this point that all you can see is the sea of blackness around you and in front of your eyes, that sea of blackness is slowly turning into individual people who are disappearing before your eyes within minutes of talking to you.

My dad stands beside me the entire time during the funeral. But through this sea of blackness, I see my mom standing at the polar opposite corner of the funeral home. My mom is a rock. She is a blond tiny five-foot-three extremely thin woman. She is the strongest person I've ever known. She will tell you the truth when you don't want to hear it. She is a woman of faith. She has a strong moral compass. She gives me a look of stern compassion as if to say, "Be strong. Get through this." And she was right. We all got through it.

*****

There is so much beauty in grief. I truly didn't understand this at the time. But it really is the truth.

When I reflect on Arash's funeral, I see I was lucky enough to have my family's and friends' support. My mother, my father, Shannon, Brendan, Sean and Ali, Diya, my Aunt Katie and Uncle Mike, my grandparents, my aunt Sue, my uncle Larry, my Uncle Danny, my Uncle Mickey and Aunt Melissa, my cousins Lauren, Kevin, Catherine, Jackie, Mikey, and Jack, and my close friends Emily, Sarah, KC, Maria, Liz, Ginny, Laura, and Elizabeth, Maureen, Megan, Nicole, Sabrina, Emily, Kristin, Julie, Terese, Shelly & John, my sister's friends Emily, Lily, Sophia, & Ryan, and many other close family friends all came to the funeral to support the Perris and I.

When my heart got heavier than I could handle, I looked to them. I saw each one of them simply being there. Not saying anything, not trying to fix anything. Not trying to say something to make it better. Just showing up. This speaks magnitudes in grief. I think too often we try to find the right words to say to someone who's going through grief. There are no right words. But your presence speaks magnitudes. There is so much power in your presence. To be there for someone in their darkest times is truly powerful.

*****

"Thank you all so much for coming. My name is Deacon Mike, and I am a close friend of the Mahers. I've been so fortunate to get to know Arash in the past year, and I would like to express my condolences to everyone in this room. I know that we have a mix of religious backgrounds in this room, from Catholic to Muslim, to everything in between. At the end of the day, we have much more in common than we have uncommon. We all believe in a good God. Arash was baptized into the Catholic faith, and I would like to share a prayer together…"

*****

"Thank you all so much for coming today. It is truly with a broken heart that I am giving this eulogy today. I hoped that I would be giving a best man's speech at a wedding." Arya began to choke up. This was the first time that I had seen Arya—quote, unquote—lose it. He had been such a pillar of strength for so long it's no surprise that this moment could be the absolute breaking point for him. But he took a deep breath, gathered his thoughts and emotions, and continued. "Arash was truly the greatest big brother I could ever ask for…"

*****

My turn. I walked up to the front of the funeral parlor; my hands were trembling. My breath was shallow. I'm not sure if my heart rate increased or decreased in this moment. I truly felt like I was going to vomit, pass out, or simply collapse. I honestly don't remember much of what I said, I don't remember much about that moment, but I do remember looking out into a crowd and I didn't recognize one face. Actually, I didn't look anyone in the eye. I purposely avoided looking directly into the sea of blackness and instead focused on the paper in front of me. The promises that we had made to each other. The love that we shared. The Arash prior to this diagnosis and the Arash during. I read from that paper as I stood next to the love of my life lying in a casket at the age of twenty-six, and I truly didn't think I would recover from this moment. I truly could feel the world stopping in that moment. I'm in the funeral procession driving alone, and outside my window, the rest of the world is standing completely still.

It's a strange feeling giving a eulogy. On one hand, you feel like you're speaking solely to the person you love whose body is now in a casket, and on the other hand, you feel like you are speaking to a room of strangers who are living in this alternate universe for the moment with you. It's so impersonal but also so personal. I blacked out during this moment. I was reading off my paper, but I had no control of what I was saying. I was "just getting through it." This blackout is different from the times I've gotten blackout drunk in college, where I'd wake up with a long list of regrets and worries. This blackout is much different. This blackout you actually feel nothing. You feel numbness. You feel trauma. You feel darkness. You feel evil. This kind of blackout is so much beyond your control that it takes years to fully recover from it.

*****

As I sit on Coronado Beach in California, a place I had first come to with Arash and his dear friends for the first time in 2020, I can hear Arash saying, "Sheesh, lighten up, Meg. It's not that serious." He's running into the water and diving into the waves, laughing at me for how dramatic I am being.

*****

Traumatic.

This day was traumatic. From beginning to end.

On my worst nights, my vision is flooded with the sea of blackness. My ears are ringing with the sounds of his family crying and mourning in Farsi. The thoughts in my brain are filled only with mourning. The constant mourning. The mourning that doesn't seem to stop even across the world. It's truly heartbreaking. The reality that is terror, war, violence, disease, abuse, and unjustness that gets passed down from generation to generation. The kind of mourning that causes your family to leave home for a better life. This trauma is so deeply engrained inside of us that we spend our entire lives trying to avoid it and ultimately rid ourselves of it.

And on my absolute worst nights, my vision is flooded with one vision, and that is of Arash in the cold, hard ground. In a brown casket. I can't shake that one. Everywhere I go. I see that. I hear that. I *am* that.

That's the thing with trauma. You can't leave it anywhere. Now it's with you everywhere you go.

*****

I didn't know this at the time, but there is so much beauty in trauma. It actually could be the most beautiful part of your life.

*****

> Ya looking for divine and the little intervention,
> & them birds don't fly, without my permission
> I'm probably in the sky, flying with the fishes
> Or maybe in the ocean, swimming with the pigeons.
> (Weezy F Baby)

Chapter 2

Just a Little Background Info

I grew up in Elmhurst, Illinois, a larger western suburb outside of Chicago, Illinois. I'm the oldest of four kids. I have two younger brothers—Brendan, twenty-seven, and Sean, twenty-two—and a younger sister, Shannon, who's twenty-four. My parents, Margaret and Bill, were both born and raised in Elmhurst, Illinois. My dad works in insurance bonds, and my mom is a paralegal. My family is an extremely tight-knit Irish-Catholic family. I went to Catholic grade school, public high school and went to the Catholic University–

Marquette in Milwaukee, Wisconsin. After I graduated with a nursing degree, I moved to Chicago for five years where I worked as a nurse at Elmhurst Hospital on a Medical-Surgical unit and then moved to the Operating Room and then a Nephrology Clinic. My closest friends are friends that I went to grade school and college with.

Arash grew up in Algonquin, Illinois, a larger northwestern suburb also outside of Chicago, Illinois. He had a brother, Arya. Both of Arash's parents were born in Iran. His father and mother were born in Iran; they moved here about thirty years ago and met in America and started a family. Arash's father has his PhD in physics and teaches college courses. Arash's mom went to cosmetology school and has her own hair salon. Arash went to public school and then graduated in 2017 from the University of Illinois with high honors, being named on a bronze tablet with his name forever engraved in the university library for graduating in the top 1 percent of the class.

Chapter 3

The Beginning

If you meet somebody and your heart pounds, your hands shake,
your knees go weak, that's not the one. When you meet your
"soul mate" you'll feel calm. No anxiety, no agitation. Just peace.

—Budhist quote

I remember it like it was yesterday.

My best friend, Emily, and I were going to the Drake concert at
the United Center in Chicago with Ryan, my friend from Marquette,
and his friend. Drake had just released a new album, and the excitement we both felt for this concert was contagious. This was at a time
in my life when I was at a low, and I was planning on moving to a
new apartment by myself, which would be my first time living alone
ever, and for that, I was especially excited for this concert. Drake
is my favorite artist at the time, and he had just recently released
his highly anticipated album, *Scorpion*. Nothing heals pain quite like
music. My friend Emily had just arrived at my Chicago apartment,
and we began to pour our typical pregame drink: a vodka, soda, lime
(called VSLs by our friends). Emily is the definition of a genuine
friend. She too comes from a very Irish, Catholic, always-boozing,
loud, rambunctious, and fun family. She has your back, gives great
advice, and truly wants what's best for everyone around her. Emily

is the life of the party. She can talk to absolutely anyone and loves to tell stories and simply enjoy the night.

It was a warm, sunny August Saturday evening in Chicago. The temperature was a perfect 75 degrees. Not a cloud in the sky. There truly is nothing better than a summer sunny Chicago night. It's what makes the bleak, freezing winters there tolerable. The vibes were high, the drinks were flowing. Emily and I were both wearing all-black tight dresses, and Drake's album was blasting in the background, and we were excited for the night ahead.

The doorbell rang. The sound was so faint compared to Drake's "God's Plan" in the background. I quickly grabbed the remote, lowered the volume, yelled to Emily "They're here!" and ran to the door in my tall black heels that I was clumsily tiptoeing around in.

I whipped the door open. Ryan walked in wearing a black-and-white striped shirt and jeans carrying a case of beer. "Hey, Meg!"

"Hey, Ryan! Come on in! We're so excited."

Ryan smiled and walked past me into our loud pregame. "This is my friend, Arash."

"Hey, nice to meet you!" Arash smiled.

Arash was gorgeous. He had these dark, striking brown Iranian eyes that pierced your heart. He had eyelashes so long it almost looked like he was wearing makeup. He was wearing a simple but sexy black T-shirt. He had thick eyebrows, thick dark hair, and perfectly tanned warm skin. He had a radiant, kind smile that was infectious. He was the kind of guy you noticed when he walked into a room. He was extremely confident in himself but not cocky. He had the sort of confidence where he was so secure in himself that he genuinely wanted everyone around him to feel that same level of confidence and self-love that he felt. He didn't boast, he wasn't prideful. He was secure and confident.

That being said, when I first gave Arash a hug soon after meeting him, I didn't have these intense butterflies or feeling of not being able to breath when I met him. I honestly felt like I was giving a hug to an old friend that I had known for forever that I just hadn't seen in a very long time.

"Who wants a drink?" Emily yelled over the loud music.

Ryan and Arash both agreed, and Emily began making drinks.

Another thing I noticed immediately about Arash was how intelligent he was. The way he spoke was unlike anyone I had ever met before. He was very worldly; he spoke with a humbleness that was extremely rare to find in men in their early twenties. When you talked to him, you knew he was different. He had experienced things that most men in their twenties hadn't. He was truly unlike anyone I had ever met before.

Ryan and Emily were talking in the living room, and Arash and I were standing in the kitchen.

"So what do you do for work?" Arash asked me. As he took a sip of his vodka soda, his gold bracelet caught my eye.

"I'm a nurse. What about you?"

"Oh, that's awesome, I'm in healthcare consulting. Maybe we could help each other out." Arash winked.

I smiled and laughed.

*****

When I look back on that night, I can't help but smile. Arash had some slick line to get my number, and naturally, I gave it to him. He had swag, personality, and he was truly the most interesting person I had ever met. He had so many hobbies, he had so many interests. He was extremely well-rounded and intelligent. I felt so comfortable with him immediately, and that's a feeling that truly never changed.

*****

"Shoot! It's almost time for the concert, I'll call an Uber," Emily gushes.

We had different seats than Ryan and Arash. Emily and I were up in the nosebleeds, and Ryan and Arash had front-row seats. That was another thing about Arash that I fell for. Being with him felt larger than life. He always had the best tickets to sporting events, concerts, you name it. He lived life to the absolute fullest; it's one of the many things I loved about him.

We piled into the Uber and then went our separate ways entering the United Center.

Chapter 4

Resistance

At the time, I had just started working as a new nurse on a medical-surgical floor at Elmhurst Hospital. I was very stressed out at the time. I was working the night shift and truly never quite adjusted to these hours. I was always exhausted, and my circadian rhythm was completely out of whack. I was eating at unhealthy times of the day and was definitely not the best version of myself. I was also about to move into a studio apartment in Chicago, and I was anxious about living alone for the first time in my life. I had always lived in a house full of siblings or roommates up until this point, and I was very worried about this. I was not looking to date. I was not looking for a relationship, and yes, I thought Arash was cute and friendly! But I wasn't interested in going out with him at the time.

"I'm taking you to dinner this week," Arash texted me.

As I mentioned earlier, Arash was extremely confident. This was enduring and inspiring, but with how low I was feeling in my own life at the time, it made the pursuit of love and his advancements even more unfavorable.

"I'm not really looking for anything," I wrote back.

*****

Driving has always been extremely therapeutic for me. I would look forward to driving to and from Marquette on holiday breaks, I commuted from Chicago to Elmhurst for work for five years, and I drove thirty hours from Chicago to California to apparently write this book. There is something so peaceful and serene about driving. I've been searching to understand why that is. I think driving has a way of making you conscious of your thoughts. It almost forces you to take the time to focus on the journey of life. You're just cruising on the highway, changing speeds as needed to keep up with the traffic, you're adjusting to changing weather climates, you're watching your speed to avoid getting pulled over, and you're driving ultimately to make it to your final destination. Also, in a sense, driving is having total control but also not having control at the same time. You sort of realize how you're only in control of your car. As much as you think you can predict what's going to happen on the road or how another car is going to drive, you truly can't. And for some reason, I find a sense of comfort in this.

God has always spoken to me the clearest when I'm driving.

I told Arash I wasn't interested in anything a few times after he asked me out on dates. But one early morning after I was driving home from an exhausting, stressful night shift back to my Chicago apartment to pass out for the day, a stronger power told me to give Arash a chance.

I really can't explain it. I just had this overwhelming feeling when I was completely exhausted and drained that I needed to give him a chance. This was very odd to me because I had met Arash about a month prior, and for a solid month, I completely wrote him off. But something told me that day to give him a chance.

Looking back on this, I think I had been running from this power my entire life up until this point. I was in a cycle of stress. I was very stressed out with my new night shift nursing job that led to a lot of binge drinking and sexual promiscuity at the time. I would deal with the stress of my job by drinking and then would wake up the next day hating myself for the mistakes I had made the night prior. I was continuously telling myself I was horrible and not worthy of any type of love or forgiveness. I definitely didn't love myself and didn't think anyone else could.

Reflecting on this, maybe that's why that higher power nudged me in Arash's direction that morning in the car.

Now, to be completely honest with you, Arash is not the person I pictured I would end up falling in love with. I grew up in Elmhurst, Illinois, a mostly white suburb. I went to Catholic grade school and Catholic college, and most of the people I knew were Irish-Catholic. I really didn't have much exposure to diverse nationalities or religions growing up. I always pictured myself ending up with someone with a similar background to me. I never in a million years pictured myself falling in love with a Persian-American man whose parents came to America from Iran, a predominantly Muslim country. Arash was not a practicing Muslim, but still, this was very out of my comfort zone. I had grown up going to Catholic school for a majority of my life, going to church every Sunday and came from a very devout Catholic family.

Growing up, I always believed in a structure of society that I had built in my head from observing my family's values, my church's values, my school's values, my community's values, etc. I had a plan for my life: I'm going to go to school and get good grades so I can become a nurse and meet and fall in love with a nice Irish Catholic man and raise a family. Reflecting now, I think most cultures have the same values at their core but just have different ways of expressing them. At the time, I could only focus on our cultural differences. But in reality, I think all cultures have waaaaaay more in common than we think.

I also think I was so caught up in what I thought I should be doing according to what societal influences were leading me to believe that I never really knew what I should ACTUALLY be doing. Subconsciously, I was living for the opinions and approvals of other people.

I truly think the first time I heard God's voice that clearly and that strongly was in the car that day when I was completely exhausted, discouraged, and drained when he told me to give Arash a chance.

And now I hear God's voice encouraging me to write this book honestly and accurately so that maybe someone out there who is grieving or in pain and is searching for any type of light in a seemingly impending dark tunnel on their own journey can relate in some way and find the strength to carry on.

Chapter 5

The First Date

She's got a smile on her, that puts a smile on me.

—"My Darling" (Lil Wayne and Drake)

Another moment I can remember like it was yesterday.

I remember talking to Arash for the first time on the phone. Soon after my revelation in the car, I texted Arash back to confirm going on a date. He didn't text me back, he called me. And we talked for two hours. We clicked instantly on the phone. We laughed and talked about music, sports, hobbies, our fun college memories, and pretty much everything in between. There wasn't a moment of hesitation or awkwardness. It was like picking up the phone and catching up with an old friend you hadn't talked to in a while. This was an amazing feeling but also a strange feeling in regards that I had only met him once prior to this.

I can still hear Arash's laugh through the other speaker of the phone. I can hear the warmness in his voice that was somehow transmitted through the phone through my veins into my soul. We just clicked. When I spoke to Arash, I felt at peace. I felt safe. I felt secure. I felt like I had finally met my other half.

"I'll pick you up at 7."

I didn't feel the usual first-date jitters that you usually encounter when going on a first date with someone you barely know. I actually felt very at ease prior to this date. The typical dread prior to going on a first date "What do I talk about? What do I wear?" fears that had always entered my mind prior to first dates did not occur at all prior to my first date with Arash. For the first time in my life, I actually was looking forward to going on a first date, not dreading it.

Arash picked me up in his slick black Volkswagen, and off we went. We went to get dinner at Naoki Sushi, an intimate romantic sushi place located in the lobby of the Lincoln Hotel in Chicago, directly across from Lincoln Park Zoo and Lake Michigan.

Arash grabbed my hand as we walked through the restaurant's kitchen to see the hostess. The waitress led us to our table, which was a cozy red booth along the window of the restaurant overlooking Lincoln Park.

I honestly think I fell in love with Arash on this first date. We talked about absolutely everything. Our chemistry was so natural and noticeable that the waiter jokingly avoided coming to our table because he "didn't want to interrupt." The instant we sat down, I felt like an adventure was about to begin. I had never had sushi before, and this excited Arash. He was thrilled to take charge and order the best things on the menu and to joyfully share this experience with me. Arash never made me feel small, ever. For as smart as he was, he could have had moments where it showed in mean, condescending ways, but never once did he make me feel like that. I didn't know how to use chopsticks on this first date, and Arash was delighted to teach me how to use them. We ordered drinks, appetizers, entrees, desserts. The whole nine yards. And shortly after, we claimed Naoki Sushi as our place. We would continue to frequent here for birthdays, Valentine's days, and other special occasions.

After the date, I truly knew that I had found my person. It was a feeling so unfamiliar to me but so exciting and refreshing. A passion was running through my veins, my love for life was reignited, and I looked forward to every morning because I couldn't wait to talk to Arash or see him next. I was eager for the next adventure with him leading the way.

Chapter 6

The Second Date

"Do you love this guy?"

—My dad

Arash's friends would joke he had a lucky horseshoe and had the "luck of the Irish." He was constantly winning drawings for games, concerts, and shows randomly. I found this pretty ironic since I actually was Irish and never had any luck winning any sort of drawing or contest.

Arash won two tickets in a random lottery drawing to go see *Hamilton* in the first row shortly after the show had come to Chicago, and he invited me to go with him. The show was new to Chicago, and this was a big deal to go see it. I was over the moon excited when he asked me to go.

"Yes! Of course!"

I remember going home to the suburbs to see my family one weekend and my dad immediately could recognize on my face that I had met someone. I sincerely had a permanent smile on my face for months after Arash and I first went out. Arash sincerely lit up my life, and it was noticeable to everyone around me how happy I was with him. My dad asked me if I loved this guy, and I couldn't help but just smile.

When you know, you know.

*****

What I would do to go back in time and have a simple moment with you. To have a cup of coffee with you, to watch a television show with you. To just sit with you. To hold your hand again. To just be with you.

Chapter 7

Love of Travel

Travel gives me life, like a man with the gavel.

—"King Kong" (Lil Wayne)

I don't think I really knew Arash until I went on my first trip with him. I feel like you learn a lot about someone when you travel with them. There's a different sense of vulnerability with traveling. Things often don't go exactly as planned. Navigating through airports and flying are stressful times. Flights can be delayed, luggage can get lost, flights can be long and uncomfortable. New hotels and new environments can be intimidating and increase anxiety. At times, it can be difficult to find your way in these new places.

Arash loved traveling with his entire soul. He was a professional. When I traveled with Arash, I sincerely felt like I was a VIP on a private tour. He took weeks to research and plan the perfect trip. He would find the best restaurants and things to do in each city we went to. He was passionate about fully immersing himself in the culture, the language, the food, the art, the history, the scenery, and the nightlife of each new city. He would have the day planned out from 6:00 a.m. to 10:00 p.m. every single day. Every day was packed with activities.

Arash traveled to so many places.

Boulder, Colorado. Austin, Texas. Washington, DC. Philadelphia, Pennsylvania. New York, New York. New Orleans, Louisiana. Milwaukee, Wisconsin. Phoenix, Arizona. Pittsburgh, Pennsylvania. Charleston, South Carolina. Nashville, Tennessee. Seattle, Washington. Detroit, Michigan. San Francisco, California. Los Angeles, California. Las Vegas, Nevada.

Playa del Carmen, Quintana Roo. Amsterdam, Netherlands. Venice, Italy. Barcelona, Spain. Bogota, Colombia. Munich, Germany. Prague, Czech Republic. Quito, Ecuador. London, England. Dublin, Ireland. Cancun, Mexico.

And his favorite: Kyoto, Japan.

And my favorite: San Diego, California.

Chapter 8

The MRI

"Megan, they found something on my MRI." Arash's voice became unsteady through the phone.

It was Friday, August 13, 2021. I will never forget this day. I was working at Elmhurst Hospital as a nurse in a nephrology clinic, and I knew that Arash was going in for an MRI of his brain that morning. Arash had a medical history of a benign brain tumor in 2015 that was successfully surgically removed. As a result, he had routine MRIs every six months to rule out any growth or reoccurrence in his brain.

This was always a stressful time for us. Correction, this was always a stressful time for *me*. Arash had the type of strength that is rare to find in a young man, and he never showed any type of outward anxiety or fear that I can only imagine he had. Looking back on it, the nights before his MRI scans were very monumental times in our relationship. Oftentimes, I would toss and turn the entire night worrying about the what-ifs and the possibilities of the next day, only to find that I worried for nothing and his MRI turned out completely unchanged.

Phew. Deep breath. And continue with the day.

This time was different. The night prior to this MRI on Friday the 13th was the first time Arash ever stated that he was worried. We sat in our home on the gray cozy broken-in couch that was passed down from my first studio apartment a few years prior.

"Meg, I don't know about this one."

I stroked Arash's thick dark hair as he laid his head down on my lap and stretched out his legs on the couch. I see the scar that ran down the left side of his skull from his first craniotomy, and my muscles tense up. The Chicago Cubs game was playing on the flat-screen TV hanging above our fireplace. Arash was the biggest Cubs fan you would ever meet. We had gone to multiple games in our relationship and had even traveled to different cities to see the Cubs play, one of which was Milwaukee a year or so prior. The Milwaukee Brewers beat the Cubs 17–4 that night.

When we got into bed that night, I knew something felt different. Something felt off. Arash had never acted this way before MRIs in the past. Usually, I was the one worrying and Arash would be talking me down and telling me he was going to be all right. He was so strong for so long it was alarming to see this change in him.

1:01 a.m. Arash is sleeping soundly, and I wake up to get a glass of water. My mind is racing. I sit at our kitchen counter in one of our royal red barstools and drink a glass of water, trying to calm my anxiety. Trying to quiet the fear that I can feel building up in my bones. I say a few prayers and go to bed. Continuing to tell myself that all the MRIs have been stable in the past, I'm sure this one won't be any different...

Chapter 9

California

There's no place like California.

I fell in love with it instantly. Everywhere around you is beauty. God's presence is everywhere you go. The winding roads, the everlasting hills, the ocean views, the sounds of one wave crashing into the next—these remind you of a hopeful, bright eternity that is waiting for you at the end of this life. The flowers and trees are so perfectly bright, so perfectly and naturally watered they almost look fake. The palm trees stand so perfectly still because there is only a very slight breeze to move the branches. The sky is the most beautiful color of bright blue, and the clouds move through the sky like they are slowly making their way to the next place. The sun is hot, but it feels good on your skin. It rejuvenates you and inspires you. California is another place where I feel God speaks the clearest to me. It's nearly impossible to not be mesmerized by the beautiful sounds echoing in your ears, the beautiful, diverse people walking around, the stunning images that fill your vision. It's easy to find yourself here, and easy to lose yourself here. Easy to be passionate, and easy to be lazy. *Lazy* in the best sense of the word. No place makes you stop and smell the roses or take in the views of the ocean to really feel the sun burning your skin quite like California.

*****

I see Arash sitting under the cherry blossom tree near the Balboa Park fountain, laughing.

"Take it easy, Meg. There's beauty everywhere."

*****

Arash passed away in the summer. His family would continue to bring flowers to his gravesite and cover it with beautiful pink, red, and yellow roses to signify new life. Mrs. Perri was extremely passionate about her beautiful garden at their home in Algonquin, and this showed in the new garden she had planted on Arash's gravesite. White butterflies would flutter over Arash's gravesite, weaving in and out of the bright colorful flowers. We always saw this as a sign that he was still with us. This was his way of communicating to us.

It took me thirty hours to drive to California. And now I see yellow butterflies.

Sometimes, I have dreams of Arash and me driving through the California hills in a blue flashy Beamer. The radio cranked high, the rooftop down, the wind blowing through our hair. I sit in the passenger seat and turn to Arash, who's driving the car. He is as healthy as can be. He smiles and grabs my hand.

I'm at peace.

Chapter 10

It'll Be Okay

As I mentioned earlier, driving has always been therapeutic for me, and the drive from Chicago to California was no different.

However, this drive was difficult. For many reasons. I knew that driving across the country would be a challenge, but honestly, it was more challenging than I imagined. I was fortunate enough to have my mother drive halfway to Colorado with me, but this was no easy feat.

My mother and I planned to wake up at 4:30 a.m. to hit the road. Naturally, neither of us slept. The anticipation of the long drive ahead of us was too much to quiet our brains and go to sleep. My mother claims she didn't sleep a wink, where I tossed and turned the entire night both eager and afraid of the journey ahead.

It was a Saturday morning. The sky was completely black, and it felt like there was no trace of life on the streets. We knew it would be dark at this early hour, but somehow this felt much darker than we anticipated. We both filled up our mugs with black Keurig coffee, gave my dad and dog, Bandit, a hug, and hit the road.

My mother is a beautiful woman; she truly is my hero. She is often told she looks and reminds others of a mix of Reese Witherspoon and Kristin Chenoweth. She is faithful, bubbly, positive, and the funniest person you'll ever meet. She is the life of the party and quite frankly my hero and biggest role model.

*****

One particular memory that stands out illustrating how strong my mother is was when I told her on Friday, August 13, that Arash was diagnosed with a brain tumor. There are just some looks you never forget. My mom's eyes filled with tears. Arash had truly become beloved by my family throughout the years, and I don't think I realized until now how much this had to have affected my mom. But she is a selfless woman, and she sat down on my bed in my childhood home and told me it was going to be okay. My father sat beside her and added, "It's pretty clear what the right thing to do here is."

I know people going through grief typically get angry when people tell them it's going to be okay. I know I did. For the first few weeks after Arash was diagnosed with brain cancer, I was angry. Angry at everyone, angry at God. How could this be happening? How could God try to take away the person that I loved the most in the world? The person I envisioned starting a life with and being with forever? I watched our friends and people we know get engaged and married. Having to forcefully smile and put on a front while attending engagement parties and weddings knowing that this was not going to happen for Arash and me. When people told me "I'm sorry" or "It's going be okay," I would internally clench my fists and think to myself, "What the hell do you know?"

But grief comes in waves. As I sit on Ocean Beach in San Diego, California, I can't help but chuckle to myself remembering when Arash first took me to this beach to go kayaking. We were horrible at it, and oftentimes, we would get pushed away by the waves from the group and have difficulty catching back up with the tour group.

There is beauty in someone telling you that it's going to be okay, even when you are furious, even when you don't want to hear it, even when you don't believe it, even when all you want to do is scream as loud as you can to release the excruciating pain raging inside you.

I say this because my mom told me on that Friday the 13th that it was going to be okay. I didn't want to hear it. I wanted to collapse into an alternate version of myself. I wanted to run until the pain stopped. I wanted to scream into the ocean that this wasn't fair. I wanted to sob for the person I loved unconditionally for four years. I wanted to shut down. I wanted to disappear and float to the bottom of the ocean.

My mom told me that it was going to be okay.

And it was.

*****

The first day of our road trip, my mom and I drove fourteen hours to Fort Collins, Colorado, to visit my cousin Jackie at Colorado State. Jackie is a beautiful college student with dark brown curly hair, beautiful blue eyes and is studying to be a veterinarian at Colorado State. We only stopped to go to the bathroom and fill up on gas. This is how my mom operates; her father was a Marine, and she definitely has the discipline of one. We encountered every weather condition possible on this drive. The first few hours, it was as dark as the blackness I once saw staring out into the crowd at Arash's funeral.

When I'm driving, I am focused. I get lost in the song that is blasting from the speaker. My thoughts go to a higher place, I think better thoughts, I am inspired, I am looking forward to the journey ahead. I am grasping on to the lyrics of songs that inspire me to move forward, not backward. We are in Iowa at this point of the drive, and I see a black car parked in the median of the highway. "Was this an undercover cop?" was my initial thought. I started to slow down, but my heart rate sped up. For a few minutes, I was completely wrapped up in the thought that this car was following me, that this car was an undercover cop car that was about to pull me over. The thoughts raced in my mind, my heart rate sped up, my breathing became heavy, and my palms started sweating. Now, I'm sure anyone reading this would think that a rational person would slow down the car, let this undercover cop pass you, and make sure you don't get pulled over and get a ticket. This was what my mind was telling me to do. I knew that this was the right thing to do in the situation, and this is what I *wanted* to do; however, my foot pushed down harder on the gas, the speed increasing to 88 mph, and I felt a loss of control overcome my body. My mind was telling me to do one thing, but my body was instinctively doing another thing.

Bright, haunting red and blue lights flashed behind us. Loud, alarming sirens started going off. My mom says, "Oh crap!" I pull over to the side of the road. My first thought upon pulling over was *This is the first few hours of the trip, and I've already gotten pulled over. This is a sign that I should not be doing this, I shouldn't be going. I need to turn around and go home. What was I thinking? Who do you think you are?*

A knock taps on the window. The sky is still completely black, and a cop approaches the car.

"Do you know how fast you were going?"

"Officer, honestly, I don't. I'm so sorry, I didn't realize how fast I was going."

"You were going 88 mph in a 55 mph zone. It took me minutes to even catch up to you. License and registration," he demands.

My mom fumbles through the glove compartment and hands the insurance card to the officer.

"This is expired."

My heart stops. Another strike. I think to myself, *Who do you think you are? You can't do this. You can't make this trip. This is a mistake. Turn around and go home right now. This cop is about to give you a ticket, and the whole trip will now be tainted from this moment on.*

"Wait here," the officer says. He takes my expired insurance card and bent Illinois driver's license to his car.

My mom must have been able to read my face because she immediately started to try to calm me down as tears began to fill my eyes. "It's going to be okay," my mom whispers.

There it is. The numbness. It came back. It filled my body from head to toe. The numbness I had felt when Arash passed away, the numbness I felt staring at his face in that casket, the numbness I felt watching his casket get lowered into the ground. All the anxiety, fear, and worry that I had felt just a few minutes previously was gone. I just felt numb. I couldn't even gather words to say to my mother.

A few minutes go by. But it felt like hours. My mother and I sat in silence.

The officer knocks on the window. "Okay, I'm going to let you go. But slow down, and be careful. You're not going to get to Colorado going 90 mph."

A wave of relief overcame my body.

*****

Arash smiles from the back seat of the car. "You can't give up that easily."

Chapter 11

The Brain Tumor

"Keep My Spirit Alive"

—Kanye West, *Donda*

After Arash's most recent MRI, his neurologist who had been handling his care up until this point took one look at the scan and told Arash he wished him the best and could no longer continue as his provider.

That is how bad the scan was.

As a nurse who had previously worked in neurosurgery, I had seen pretty bad MRIs of patients' brains. But this was unlike anything I had ever seen.

*****

The clock was ticking ever so slowly on the wall as Arash, his parents, and I sat in the doctor's office at Northwestern Hospital awaiting to speak to the neurologist. The walls were painted white; there were little to no paintings on the wall. Mr. Perri paced the room back and forth while Mrs. Perri and I sat on the small firm brown futon. Arash sat at a smaller desk right next to me in a wooden chair. The couch felt like no one had ever really sat on it before. It was firm and cold. The all-white walls were deafening in their own way, and our backs faced an absolutely gorgeous view of Lake Michigan and the tall buildings in the Gold Coast of Chicago. However, this view didn't look gorgeous that day. The city that I once saw so beautifully was completely altered in my mind. The city where Arash and I had met, had explored, had fallen in love in had made our home seemed cold and distant. August 25, 2021. It was a beautiful summer, sunny day in Chicago, but it felt like a below-freezing-temperature winter day to me. It's as if there was a blizzard outside that only I could see.

Minutes pass, the silence in the room is deafening. No one said a word. Arash and I exchanged soft smiles and held hands, but no words were exchanged. We were just waiting. There was nothing to say.

"Good morning. My name is Dr. B. Nice to meet you all." Dr. B was a tall, skinny middle-aged white man. To be honest, I don't remember much about him at all.

Dr. B pulled up the MRI. It showed Arash's brain in a white tracing with a huge black mass covering both lobes. You didn't have to be a healthcare professional to take one look at this MRI and know that it was bad news. Dr. B explained to us that the tumor was growing, and it was growing quickly.

*****

This MRI reminded me of a sad, lifeless painting. Looking at it, you couldn't come to one good conclusion. It was black and white. Life versus death. Good versus evil. There was nothing to learn from it. It was what it was. The prognosis was bad. And there were very little medical interventions to stop it from progressing.

*****

"You have options. We have a clinical trial that is starting for patients with brain tumors..."

My mind drifted. I stopped listening to the doctor. His lifeless, impersonal words began to numb my ears. All I could think about was trying to keep things the exact same. To choose any option that would keep Arash here with me for as long as possible. Any option to keep him the same, to keep his warm personality, his contagious laugh, his love for life here on earth with me. In that moment, I didn't care about clinical trials or advancing science. I didn't care about anything except Arash.

*****

For a long time, I resented Northwestern. I was angry with the way they presented the clinical trial to Arash, like they were selling him a car and they were giving him a good deal.

This caused a lot of confusion for me. I worked as an operating room nurse in surgery for two years prior. My specialty was neurosurgery. I had seen mistakes made in surgery by surgeons who were ranked the top among their peers. Granted, this was rare, but seeing routine surgeries changing to life-threatening surgeries before your eyes sticks with you and influences your views as you sit on the other side of the medical conversation.

Ultimately, the decision was made as a family after many, many conversations were had about the best way to move forward.

Long story short, the risks of the clinical trial outweighed the benefits with Arash's poor prognosis, and the decision was made not to participate in the clinical trial and instead to continue down the traditional route of chemotherapy.

Chapter 12

California Part 2

I never really appreciated art before. I never really understood it. I always figured it was too fancy and upscale for my standards. I got bored easily in museums. I figured art was for the most fortunate people to waste money on and have meaningless conversation on.

My mind has completely changed. Art is basically everywhere. It's everything. It's everywhere you go. It's universal.

In the last few months of Arash's life, I spent so much time at the Perris. Their house was absolutely beautiful. They had Persian rugs that lined the floors and the walls, some with beautiful, vibrant colors and others with soft, comforting colors. They had throw pillows that were traced with gorgeous beads and endless flowers that lined their windowsills. They had colorful paintings on the walls and there were no empty spaces in their home. Every centimeter was covered with either a rug, a trinket, a flower—you name it. They always had pistachios and a variety of fruits out for guests. And Persian tea was always flowing, whether you wanted it or not.

I've learned that it is Persian culture to serve and dote on their guests the entire time. The Perri's were overly generous and always kind.

*****

Art is only seen as fancy, upper class, or pompous because humankind has a tendency to make it to be. There is art in the way the tiles are arranged on the ground, there is art in the way water perfectly spouts from a fountain, there is art in the way particles of color merge together so that we can see a bigger picture. There is art in a bride's wedding dress as each piece of fabric is perfectly woven together to make the final dress. There is art in a groom's wedding suit as each line was perfectly woven to create the final project.

I don't see art in the same way as I did before. Art is universal, it's the story of how certain things happen in different orders so a bigger picture can be created and appreciated. Art is the tangible proof of the continuation of God's plan. We as people are ever evolving, ever adjusting, and ever changing.

*****

I can hear Arash laughing at me once again. "Take it easy, Picasso."

Chapter 13

The Seizure

Arash's seizures seemed to blend together. I can't honestly tell you when the first one was. Some were short, quick, and only took minutes for Arash to regain control. Some lasted longer and required medical attention. Some occurred at Northwestern while he lay in a hospital bed, some occurred while he was playing basketball with his friends, some occurred at our home while we were sitting on our favorite gray comfy couch.

Seizures are odd. No one seems to know what causes them. There are medications to help stop them once they've started or to decrease the severity of them while they're occurring, but medicine still can't give you a solid answer as to what actually causes them. Sure, alcohol, flashing lights, dehydration, stress, and lack of sleep can trigger them. But no one actually knows what causes them.

One seizure really sticks out in my mind. It was a weeknight in December; it was a typical frigid, cold night in Chicago. We were sleeping in our bed, and suddenly, I was awakened by Arash's shaking body. He is having a massive tonic-clonic seizure where his entire body is jerking. His muscles are stiffening and twitching. His body is viciously jerking the bed up and down. I scream in horror.

"Arash!"

I immediately jumped out of bed and turned the lights on. But this didn't stop. It continued for five minutes, which felt like much longer than that at the time. I was utterly horrified. I immediately called 911.

Shortly after, I see red bright lights glaring from our living room window and hear the alarming sounds of the sirens echoing off our bedroom walls. Arash is still in a seizure, and for five minutes, my soul left my body. All I could see were the red lights of the ambulance. They were so bright they pierced my vision. All I could hear was Arash's body jerking up and down on the bed, and the loud sirens were piercing my eardrums. I still to this day have never witnessed anything so terrifying. I thought Arash was about to die. I wasn't prepared, I wasn't ready. I had no idea what to do except exist and wait for EMT to arrive.

Four burly men burst into our apartment and ran into our bedroom. Shortly after they arrived, Arash's body stopped jerking, and he came to. He was back.

"Oh, man, you're the kid from the basketball court the other day?" one of the EMTs asked.

Arash had a seizure a few days prior while he was playing basketball with his friends. This warranted a 911 call and an emergency room visit, and it seems as if it was the same EMT team from that day that had come to our house that night. I still remember the sorrow in that officer's eyes. It reminded me of one of the looks Arash's buddies gave me when they first heard about the diagnosis. Arash was truly loved, and I really think even the EMTs could see that.

Chapter 14

California Part 3

La Jolla Beach in San Diego, California, is an incredibly stunning place to be writing this book. I think grief has a unique way of forcing us to see the world in a different way. I've sat at the beach multiple times prior to this moment. But I can confidently say I've never seen the beach quite the way I do in this exact moment.

The California hills that reside over La Jolla Cove to my left and the California hills that reside over the northern part of this state to my right look as if they are paintings. Works of art that seem to surround you on both sides and give you no choice but to move forward and look into the depths of the ocean. The ocean has a unique way of making your problems seem insignificant. My grandmother told me this, and I never quite fully understood it. Whatever is weighing heavy on your heart, whatever challenge seems impossible, whatever pain you are holding on to, when you look to the ocean and you see the infinity of it all, those problems slowly fade in your brain. They seem to take up less space as you let the infinity of the ocean dominate them.

Grief has taught me that this is a learned brain mechanism. It's not natural. It's a constant conscious decision that you have to make every day to refocus your thoughts on infinity, not on the problems, hangups, pain, trauma, and stress that is in the world around you.

I know this isn't easy. It wasn't easy for me for an extremely long time. It still isn't. I battled with the demons of grief and loss for what seemed like eternity while Arash was sick and after he died, and I still am battling those fears slowly every day.

Every day gets a little easier. On some days, it seems impossible to believe that God is good. That the world is a good place. That there is something to look forward to at the end of all this. But sitting right now in this moment, staring into the beautiful red, orange, and yellow rays that are reflecting off the constantly moving, constantly changing, constantly adapting waves of the ocean, I've never been more aware that God is good. Life is good. There is something to look forward to despite all the challenges of this world that are surrounding you.

It might just take some time to get there.

Chapter 15

Rain

Cliffs of Moher, Ireland

After driving through a few hours of darkness, the sun began to slowly rise on the horizon of the highway but was soon swept away by the February clouds of the Midwest. My mom's favorite band, Fleetwood Mac, was playing on the radio, and we were on a high after getting a pass from that officer. Gas station coffee was streaming through our bloodstream, but then the rain began.

The rain would come and go in waves. First it would be a slight drizzle barely enough to make a difference in your vision driving, but then it would pour heavily. The roads were slick, vision was minimal, and the car windshield wipers were working at double time to keep up with the pouring rain. Suddenly, the fear started to creep into my memory. My mind was transported to the day of Arash's funeral, and that pouring rain brought my mind to another place. I tried to suppress this fear and keep my eyes on the road. We were driving through Nebraska at this point, and I was determined to stay on our time track. We spent a few hours driving through this rain, and my mother offered multiple times to drive or suggested that we pull over. However, I declined.

Similar to the undercover cop situation, I had another situation where my mind was telling me to do the rational thing, but I could feel my body declining this order and telling my mind to change and adapt. Sure, we could pull over and wait for the rain to pass, but there was no promise when/if that would happen. It was completely out of our control, and I felt a slight peace come over me.

It wasn't in my control, so I wasn't going to worry about it. Regardless of whether I pulled over to the side of the road or kept driving, the circumstances were still the same. The rain was out of our control. I decided to trust my gut and allow my mind to change. I listened to this and drove at a reasonable speed, keeping my focus on the road, giving space to the cars in front of me and behind me and continued driving. We would get through this.

*****

There's nothing quite like rain in Ireland.

The only reason I can even write that above statement is because Arash took me there in 2019. As I mentioned, Arash loved to travel, it was his fiercest passion in life. He was extremely open-minded and the least-judgmental person you would ever meet. He genuinely loved learning about other places and cultures. When Arash landed in a new city, you could see the spark ignite in his eyes. He was about to go experience absolutely all that he could in that new city: the food, the people, the art, the music, the history, the nightlife. He would learn something new from this new place, and he would carry it with him to the next. And he would become better from it.

Arash would take weeks to plan the perfect trip. He did research to find the greatest places to eat, the best tours to go on, the main attractions you had to see in each city and would actively search for the hole-in-the wall places that would ensure you really got the "local feel" on the trip.

Ireland was no different. Like all other trips we had gone on, Ireland was an adventure. Ireland stands out to me as my favorite trip for obvious reasons, but I still remember the feeling of stepping off that plane into Ireland. It was raining lightly.

But this rain felt different. It felt warm, it felt comforting, like it had been waiting for you. Like it was giving you a hug and welcoming you back. Even though I had never been to Ireland previously, stepping off that plane in Ireland, I truly felt like I had. Similar to the feeling I had when I met Arash for the first time.

No anxiety, no agitation. Just peace.

*****

I can see Arash's face sipping on a Guinness across the pub table from me as he grabs my hand. His smile lightens up the rainy day.

Chapter 16

The Brain Surgeries

Arash's health was deteriorating. He began to lose his vision, he lost his ability to talk, his ability to walk. His seizure medications weren't working anymore. The doctors tried adjusting his medications, but this was unsuccessful.

Arash moved back to his parents' house in Algonquin, Illinois, because he needed more care than could be provided at our home in Chicago.

Arash had two brain surgeries during his journey. One happened soon after his diagnosis, which was done to remove the part of the tumor that deemed safe to remove without making any of his complications worse.

The second surgery occurred while Arash was on hospice care. This surgery was done to place a stent in his brain to relieve the pressure so his symptoms weren't as uncomfortable.

*****

This is the hardest part of the book to write thus far. I ask for your patience and forgiveness while I break down for a minute.

There is truly nothing more painful than watching someone so young, so vivacious, so full of life, so healthy, and so eager lose these qualities over time. The man whom I had traveled the world with, ran around Chicago with, enjoyed countless laughs with, cried with, fought passionately with, made love with was losing the ability to do all these things. One by one. And it was completely out of anyone's control. All you could do was watch. All you could do was sit and watch him die and watch his family mourn. My eyes still well up and my heart still stings if I think about this for too long.

*****

I am walking through a pretty garden in California. I don't know where it is. But it's beautiful. There are pink roses surrounding me. The fresh air breezes through my hair. The sun shines onto my skin, igniting my soul. And just like that, a yellow butterfly lands on my shoulder.

Phew. Deep breath. Continue on.

*****

Mr. Perri, Arya, and I had a meeting with the neurosurgery team prior to Arash's surgery. I learned that it is Persian culture not to involve the patient in this conversation. It was best if we spoke outside Arash's hospital room regarding his upcoming surgery.

I worked as a nurse in neurosurgery for two years while I was dating Arash. I loved it. The fast-paced environment, the teamwork, the instant gratification. Stakes are high. Egos are big. Everyone is working toward one goal. It's a fascinating place.

It's a completely different feeling when your loved one is the one going through surgery. You feel completely helpless and completely out of control.

*****

Arya, his dad, and I sat in the hallway of Northwestern Hospital. Each of us was in our own chair in a circle with the team of physicians that were about to operate on Arash. They began to explain the benefits and risks of this procedure.

"This is a routine surgery to relieve some of the uncomfortable symptoms Arash is experiencing, but as with all surgeries, there are some risks…"

My mind drifts again… I focus on the bright lights that are hanging above us in the hallway of the hospital. My mind drifts back to the operating room with all its piercing bright lights. Lights that I had never truly looked up at. Not the way a patient looks up at these lights when they're wheeled into surgery on their back, awaiting anesthesia, following anesthesia's commands to count backward from 5…4…3…2…

Arya and Mr. Perri began to shake the doctor's hand, and we walked back to Arash's hospital room.

The next morning was Arash's surgery. Arya and I accompanied him down to the pre-op surgery area following a member of the surgery team. I vividly remember that moment, more so than any of the other moments in the hospital. Arash wasn't really able to communicate with us at this point. He could give us a thumbs-up, but that was about it.

Giving a thumbs-up was Arash's staple when he could no longer communicate with us. Despite that, Arash would respond with a thumbs-up whenever you asked him a question or made a remark. His strength during that time still inspires me to this day.

*****

I often think about how different it could have been if Arash had not been so strong, so kind, so thankful, and so forgiving during this time. He had every right to be angry, mean, or unhappy, but he had the strength of a seasoned warrior. Not once did I ever hear him complain about his situation or ask, "Why me?" or say, "This isn't fair." Not once. I say that with complete honesty.

*****

We waited in pre-op for what seemed like eternity when, in reality, we probably waited about thirty minutes. Grief has a weird way of morphing your sense of time. Seconds can seem like minutes. Minutes like hours. Hours like days. Days like months. Months like years.

We listened to music the entire time we were waiting in pre-op. I held Arash's hand, and Arya cracked jokes with Arash. He continued to give a thumbs-up. Some of the most genuine laughs of my life were in this moment.

The surgery team had arrived to take Arash. The surgery team pulled Arya to the side and asked him how to proceed if the surgery took a wrong turn.

Arya's strength during this moment was unlike anything I had ever seen before. How do you even answer that question? How do you even wrap your mind around having to make that decision for your twenty-six-year-old brother? What do you even say? How do you answer that question without completely breaking down?

One thing that stands out in my mind on the morning of Arash's surgery was the genuine look of sadness on the surgery team's face. After working in surgery, I know this is not common. When the pre-op team comes to get you for surgery, they are encouraged and confident that this surgery is no big deal, that the patient will be fine.

I have been a nurse for six years, and I have never seen a doctor look at a patient the way the surgeon looked at Arash.

Arash was so completely and perfectly loved.

*****

A yellow butterfly accompanies Arash as the surgery team wheels him back to the operating room.

Chapter 17

Consciousness

After the rain in Nebraska, we reach the last stretch of our drive for the day. My mom and I enter Colorado while drinking Red Bulls and snacking on Twizzlers. Still only stopping to fill up the tank with gas or to use the restroom. Colorado was absolutely stunning. When we first arrived in the state, there was a slight snowfall as we drove through the winding roads and beautiful mountains. As we drive up these beautiful winding roads, the elevation starts climbing.

The snowfall stopped. And slowly, the sun began to peek through the layer of clouds that it literally felt like we were driving into. This was so beautiful. As the elevation climbs, we soon become extremely conscious of our breathing. Our breathing slows, and the joy settles in. After us having a rough few hours of difficult driving, the sun was finally shining.

Crank the music up!

This view of Colorado was truly one of the most beautiful things I had ever seen. It was unique in the sense that as you were driving up into the clouds if you looked to your left you would see the sun shining, and if you looked to your right, you would see stormy clouds.

Just as the elevation in the mountains forces you to be conscious of your breathing, I felt the elevation also forced me to become more conscious of my thoughts. I made a conscious decision to focus on the sun shining on the left side of the highway, allowing it to take up more space in my brain than the fear of the storm clouds on the right side of the highway.

*****

We arrive safely to Colorado and have a lovely night with my cousin Jackie.

Chapter 18

Baptism Part 1

Religion.

It's so multifaceted, so complicated, so beautiful, so helpful, so necessary but also so painful and so divisive.

Faith.

It's everything.

I want to be completely transparent. I was no perfect Catholic growing up. As you have read, I have made plenty of mistakes in my life. I have broken many church rules and at times in my life have lived in ways opposing the laws of the Catholic Church.

I grew up in a family that was Catholic, and these values had been passed on for generations and generations from Ireland. I had attended Catholic grade school and Catholic college. My grade school went to Catholic Mass every Friday, and my family went to Catholic Mass every Sunday. I studied religion at Immaculate Conception Grade School and took theology courses at Marquette. Catholicism was as much imbedded in my veins as the blood that flows from my heart to my brain.

Arash grew up in a family that had traveled from Iran, a predominantly Muslim country. But as he would tell me, they were no longer practicing Muslims. When Arash talked to me about Iran, he spoke with many mixed feelings and emotions. He would tell me about how beautiful the country was. He would describe the beautiful mosques. The floors were lined with beautifully sown Persian rugs that included beautiful bright and inspiring colors. The walls were covered with stained glass windows, and the lights would shine into these mosques, and the lights would bounce from window to window, illuminating the mosque. They had tall, high ceilings. He described the beautiful nature in Iran. The tall mountains, the dunes of sand in the desert, the beautiful greenery and flowers. The beautiful towers, the beautiful people.

He would also tell me about the violence in Iran. He told me how religion had been such a root cause of so much violence, oppression, and division in their country. It had caused horrible wars there. If you were caught breaking the laws in Iran, the consequences were awful. You could be fined, publicly flogged, arrested, or imprisoned. Alcohol was strictly prohibited, and if you were caught with alcohol, you could be publicly whipped.

This was shocking to me. Ignorantly, I was unaware of how truly severe the punishment for breaking both religious and governmental laws was in Iran.

Mr. Perri is an extremely intelligent, kind man. He is a professor of physics at multiple universities across the Chicagoland area. When our families would spend time together while Arash was sick, he would have in-depth conversations with my father and Deacon Mike about the Shah's ruling in Iran from 1953 to 1979. This was a secular and authoritarian rule, and Mr. Perri and members of his family escaped this ruling and came to America to escape the violence and division that was occurring in Iran.

Mr. Perri was part of the group working to overthrow the violent ruling of the Shah in Iran. He had served in the war and finished his schooling in Iran and traveled to America for a better life where he met Mrs. Perri and started a family.

It was interesting and fascinating to see and hear this perspective. Growing up, I always actuated religion with being the answer to all problems, not the cause of them.

To hear the traumatic stories of how war, violence, disease, torture, and murder were the root reason of why Mr. Perri moved to America for a better life was truly moving.

*****

I am standing in Mrs. Perri's garden in the gazebo that Mr. Perri built with his bare hands, sharing a meal with Arash. He is healthy, he is dancing, he is smiling. He is full of life. Yellow butterflies engulf the gazebo. The lights from the candles illuminate the gazebo with hope.

*****

God whispers to us in our pleasures, but shouts
to us in our pains.
(C. S. Lewis)

The hopelessness that is a terminal diagnosis is excruciatingly painful. To hear a neurologist at Northwestern—the best hospital in Illinois, one of the top 10 hospitals in the nation—tell you that there is nothing they can do to stop this from progressing has a way of robbing you of everything. Your future, your plans, your hope.

We were low. So low. It felt as if the doctor just told us there was a black hole in front of us and eventually you will need to step into that hole. There's no choice. There are no options. Just death. That's it.

I tried to stay positive. I said things I didn't truly believe at the time. I tried to do what was right. I was going through the motions. I felt nothing, I didn't know how to comfort Arash. I repeated to Arash what my parents told me that Friday, August 13th: "It's going to be okay." I didn't believe this. But I didn't know what else to say.

"Meg."

Arash rarely talked about the diagnosis. He was tough and strong and truly continued to live life normally. He continued to travel, continued to go to sporting games, continued to see family and friends. He didn't want this diagnosis to define him or the rest of his life. This was the only time I can truly say we talked about the depths of the diagnosis and the mortality of it all.

"You see sunshine and rainbows, and all I see is blackness and nothing."

*****

A white butterfly stops fluttering. Its wing is broken. It falls to the earth. It weeps in pain. It can no longer fly.

Chapter 19

Baptism Part 2

You don't know that God is all that
matters until God is all you got.

—Rick Warren

When everything is taken from you, you have no choice but to sit and look God in the eye & have a gut-level honest conversation. You speak with Him about everything. Every mistake you've made, every shortcoming you have, every time you've wronged someone, everything you have done in the darkness. There is no hiding anymore. You don't have the luxury of running anymore. You tell Him everything. It pours out of you. Like a heavy downpour of rain that is flooding the streets and pouring into the sewer at the end of the road. You have no choice.

Arash and I had gone to Church before. He would celebrate Christmas and Easter with my family.

*****

Chicago, Illinois

I can see Arash sitting at my parents' house on Easter Sunday. He is smiling. He is sitting in the brown recliner at my parents' house. This is his spot. He has his U of I blanket with him, and our small white fluffy dog, Bandit, is licking Arash's face and wagging his tail. He gives a thumbs-up.

*****

I was hesitant to ask Arash if he wanted to meet our family friend, Deacon Mike. It was a touchy situation, and I didn't want to upset him or force any beliefs on him. But like I said, God is all we had. There were no other options. Nowhere else to turn.

Arash agreed, and we invited Deacon Mike to our apartment that week.

Chapter 20

Baptism Part 3

Deacon Mike is a Catholic deacon who preaches at Visitation Church in Elmhurst, Illinois. He officiates marriages, funerals, and speaks at Mass. He is truly a man of God. He is kind and faithful and has a beautiful family.

He sits on our comfy gray broken-in couch from our first apartment and starts speaking to Arash. Deacon Mike has a way of making you gracefully aware of God's presence. He has a calm, kind, open demeanor. He is not judgmental, he is relatable.

I don't remember the details of that conversation. And I sincerely don't believe the details really mattered. But I remember the impact. I remember feeling at ease. Feeling at peace. I sat next to Arash and held his hand. His eyes were kind. His smile was warm. He was actively listening to Deacon Mike.

"Do you want to get baptized?"

Arash was a strong-willed man. He was confident and secure. He was passionate, and he went after what he wanted. He never gave up. He worked hard. He graduated in the top 1% at University of Illinois. He was not the type of man to compromise his values or beliefs. He was a great brother, a great son, a great friend. He would never agree to do something that he didn't believe in. In fact, he would only do things that he truly believed in, truly was passionate about, truly loved.

"Yes."

Deacon Mike gracefully poured holy water on to Arash's forehead. The water seeped through his thick dark hair. The water was cleansing. Like heavy rain that was flooding on the streets of California wiping every mistake, every pain, every holdup, every darkness, every mistake, every fear into the sewer at the end of the road.

Deacon Mike blessed a beautiful brown rosary and gave it to Arash.

After Deacon Mike left, Arash and I laid in our bed holding hands. Arash fell asleep. It was the most peaceful moment I can remember about this whole experience. I laid with my head on his chest. That tension that I had once felt in him, the rapid, abnormal heartbeat, had slowed to a peaceful rhythm. & we slept.

Chapter 21

Fog

Second day of the drive.

The plan was to drive from Colorado to Richfield, Utah, while dropping my mother off at the Denver airport on the way.

We woke up at 8:00 a.m. and hit the road. It was another tough day of driving. The rain began again, and there was a fog advisory in place in the state of Colorado. The visibility was brutal. The layer of fog was so thick you couldn't even see the car in front of you. Your senses were heightened as you had to focus on the road ahead.

Now, I have never driven in Colorado before. I'm aware that this dangerous weather condition could be nothing out of the ordinary for people who typically drive in this state. It changed my perspective. Something typical for someone in this state was causing me complete and utter fear. It was the fear of the unknown. I had never driven in such fog before, and my body didn't know how to adapt. I listened to the rational thoughts in my mind. Drive at a reasonable pace, do not take your eyes off the road, keep your lights on, and keep an appropriate distance between cars.

This put things in perspective for me. Being from Chicago, driving in snow wasn't a huge deal. We had become so accustomed to these common hazardous conditions it didn't strike the same level of fear in me that this type of unknown snow and fog did. But learning to drive in Chicago snow was a learned brain mechanism. It didn't happen overnight. In fact, I'm sure that the first time I drove in snow,

I was absolutely terrified. But because it had been so long since this first initial fear occurred, I think my subconscious buried this fear until I was forced to face it again for the first time again. Grief has a way of making you think about what you're thinking about. You're almost forced to evaluate the decisions you've made, the circumstances you've been handed in life and the ones you have created for yourself and analyze them. You ask yourself: "How did this happen?" "Why did this happen?" "What could I have done to prevent this from happening?" "How could I have stopped this from happening?"

For a long time, I truly believed God was punishing me for mistakes I had made in the past. I believed he was angry at me for my poor decisions and selfishness and this was his way of making it even with me.

But after driving in that thick fog for the first time and not being able to see what lay ahead of me, I have realized this too was a learned brain mechanism. This fearful and self-loathing feeling came from generations of trauma, violence, war, disease, pain, suffering. This is universal. It's in every culture, every place. Generations of people have left where they have come from to avoid it, to do anything it takes to not look this fear in the eye because fear is truly blinding. Fear prevents you from being who you were made to be. It's a prison of trying to please others, trying to stick to the status quo, trying to avoid facing your mistakes instead of learning and growing from them.

I made a conscious decision while driving in that thick fog that I am not going to let this fear become the main idea that occupied my brain. I focused on the destination. I took deep breaths, and like choosing the sun over the clouds while first driving into Colorado, I would choose the certainty of eternity as opposed to the fear of the present moment driving through this thick fog. Recognizing that this thick fog was out of my control, I took many deep breaths and continued to drive.

*****

The white butterfly with the broken wing lies on the ground; it can no longer fly. It hops forward with its strong hind legs and continues searching.

*****

I drop my mom off at the Denver airport. My mom is a strong woman. I can count on one hand the times I've seen her cry or become emotional. She has four kids and loves them with an intense loyalty. My mom starts to cry at the airport while she says goodbye. She gives me a hug and apologizes. "I promised myself I wasn't going to do this."

My heart breaks. Fear and uncertainty creep in. I give my mom a hug while my eyes fill with tears. She takes her suitcase and closes the car door.

I am numb. The deafening numbness sets in. But I am driving at an airport, so I had no choice but to continue driving, to make way for the driver behind me who was about to drop their loved one off at the airport. So I drive.

For about twenty minutes, I am extremely upset. I don't know how to feel. I feel numb. The numbness is deafening. "Do I call my mom? Do I turn this car around?" "What are you doing?" "Who do you think you are?" "You can't make this trip on your own."

The fog persists. I am driving into the intense fog that I just experienced with my mom, but now I am alone. Anxiety, fear, uncertainty, and numbness return, except this time the numbness feels different from the numbness in the past.

This numbness is not the joy leaving my body, never to return again. The numbness I felt at Arash's funeral. This numbness was transformative. Instead of particles leaving my body, I felt particles *changing* in my body. I again was made to be conscious of the decision I was making in that moment. The decision to leave somewhere I was comfortable and safe to try something new. To go somewhere I wasn't comfortable. I was conscious of the journey that it took to get to this moment. It was a learned brain mechanism. It wasn't overnight. Grief had changed my brain. For a long time, grief caused sadness, pain, suffering, and uncertainty. It caused me to continue in a cycle of making poor decisions, hating myself for it, and feeling like I had no other choice but to return to the cycle. Like you are in the ocean swimming to the top to get that breath but just when you're about to get there, the strong waves and hold of the ocean pull you back down a few notches. And you're still stuck.

As these twenty minutes passed, I continued to drive. I had no choice. Slowly but surely, the fog dissipated, the sun began to peek through the clouds to shine, and I could see the road again.

I texted my mom. "Sun is shining. Love you."

*****

The white butterfly continues to hop along on its hind legs in search of another butterfly.

Chapter 22

The Abbey

Soon after Arash had moved back to his parents' home in Algonquin, my family planned a trip to go to the Abbey Resort in Lake Geneva, Wisconsin, as a weekend getaway. Arash loved to travel, and not being able to anymore was truly weighing heavy on his heart. We went over St. Patrick's Day weekend. My mom, my dad, and my brother Sean drove up in one car, and Arash, Arya, and I in another car.

The drive was easy. A quick hour-and-a-half drive, and we had made it to Lake Geneva.

At this point, Arash could no longer walk or talk. He was in a wheelchair and could only communicate to us by giving a thumbs-up.

Looking back on that weekend, I see it was one of the most joyful weekends of my life. The seven of us ate dinner at one of the restaurants that overlooked the beautiful Lake Geneva. We went swimming in the resort's indoor pool and sat outside at the resort's rustic bonfires. Every night that weekend ended the same: the seven of us would sit in my parents' hotel room watching March Madness basketball games on mute. We would play Arash's favorite hip-hop songs on the speaker, and we drank Guinesses to celebrate St. Patrick's Day. We laughed. Arash laughed. He gave his infamous thumbs-up as we watched the basketball games, rooting on our bracket teams. Arya shared stories of Arash from their childhood, and we all laughed and smiled.

To this day, it is still one of my greatest memories. We were so joyful in spite of everything that was happening. We had each other, and familiarity of the basketball games on TV, the hip-hop music playing in the background, the taste of a cold Guinness, and the presence of the people you loved the most in the world filled my heart with lasting joy. For moments, it seemed like Arash wasn't sick anymore. He was going to make it. He wasn't going anywhere. He was staying here with us in that moment, in that hotel room, laughing and smiling for eternity.

*****

The broken white butterfly finds another butterfly on its path.

*****

After a joyful and fun weekend at the Abbey, it was time to go. We packed up the car, except this time only Arash and I drove back to Illinois. I drove, and Arash sat in the passenger seat. I became used to comfortable silence. Arash couldn't talk to me anymore, but it was okay. I turned the music on, and we drove back to Illinois.

Halfway through the drive, the chemotherapy that Arash had been taking combined with the motion sickness of the car made him sick.

In this moment, I realized how sick Arash really was. The fantasy that we had been experiencing all weekend came to a screeching halt. The feelings that I had experienced all weekend, the joy, the love, the laughter faded from my mind. And the reality of this sickness crept to the front of my mind. It was consuming and overwhelming. I was brought back down to earth. Arash's cancer was real. His brain was deteriorating, and he was not getting better.

*****

The white butterfly takes the other butterfly with its wings.

Chapter 23

California Part 4

The first time I came to San Diego was with Arash and his best friends, Mitch and Maris. It was my favorite place we ever traveled. As I sit and write this in the nature of San Diego, I can safely say it is still my favorite place.

There's something about California that makes you feel like you can be whoever you want. You come here, and you leave that old self behind. I was a nurse in Chicago, but I can be a writer here. You also realize life moves on. When your world stops, the rest of the world continues. The palm trees stay the same, the sun still shines the next morning, the sun still sets the next evening. You find your favorite place here, and the next day when you come back to that place, someone else is there, forcing you to find a new favorite place, allowing you to get a different perspective than you had before.

*****

My favorite photo of Arash is a photo of him sitting at Sunset Cliffs. He is wearing a Cubs jersey and black sunglasses. The setting sun beams on his face, illuminating his smile.

This was the most intimate moment I've ever shared with Arash. We were sitting at Sunset Cliffs; the pink-and-red-colored sky was the background to the sun setting over the infinite ocean. The waves were crashing again and again against the rocks at the bottom of the cliffs. We didn't speak. We just sat. We just existed. We felt at peace. We felt like this moment was never going to end. Like our whole life was leading up to this perfect, peaceful moment.

The sun sets, and we go home.

*****

The white butterfly takes the wounded butterfly on its back, and they begin to fly.

Chapter 24

Once a Week

I sincerely hope I can do this chapter justice as to how great Arash's friends and family were and as to how much they helped us get through this dark, difficult time. Arash had numerous friends. He kept in touch with them almost daily, and they shared common values, interests, and hobbies. While Arash was healthy, we spent many weekends with these friends, laughing and creating memories together in Chicago.

When Arash moved back home to be on hospice care, it was devastating. A twenty-six-year-old on hospice care? That's just not right.

Without fail, Arash's core group of friends—Mitch and Maris, Carly and Jeremy, Zach, Nicky and Evan, Ryan and Eileen, Mario and Andrea, Enrique and Vanessa, Amar, Kara and Dane, Jon, Natalie and Sam, Nikki and Zvonko, Tom, Joe, and Sam—would drive from the city during rush hour traffic every single week, bringing food, positive energy, laughs, stories, and joy. They came once a week every week until Arash passed. Without fail. There wasn't a single week they didn't show up.

Arash's cousins—Suhail, Sheiva, Farbhod, Mehron, Bobby, Ashkhan, Keon, Sean, Suha, Sahand, Farheed, Amir, Fariba, Lina and Mikey, and Romina—would show up to the Perris almost daily in the last few months of Arash's life.

This was truly beautiful. There is so much beauty in community. There is beauty in numbers. I don't remember all that we talked about. I don't remember all the jokes or the stories or the words of encouragement they gave to Arash, his family, and me. But I remember them showing up every single week. Without fail. I remember how I could rely on this. I remember how much I looked forward to this. This was a sense of community, a sense of belonging. For a moment, Arash wasn't sick anymore. He was completely healed.

*****

The white butterflies become one and go on to fly and meet new butterflies.

*****

There is strength in community. There is strength in presence. There is strength in this kind of dependability.

Chapter 25

Arash Passes, Part 1

The days leading up to Arash passing away were excruciating.

I had taken a leave from work and was driving to the Perri's every morning for a few months before Arash passed. I had a routine. I would wake up, run a few miles, eat a healthy breakfast, go to Protein Bar to get a shake for Arash, because that is all he could consume at this point, and I would drive to the Perri's every day.

There's beauty in routine. I think there's necessity to it. It's foundation. The discipline of doing the same thing over and over again makes you strong. It isn't until you're suffering that you realize how strong you are. Yes, I was going through the motions at this time. I was in a dark place. Everything we did to make Arash better was failing. The medicine, the doctor's appointments, the chemotherapy, the fun outings we planned, the family gatherings. We kept trying to change the situation that was unfolding in front of us, but it wasn't changing. It was out of our control.

I remember how important it was to me to continue to run. It was my therapy. My stress relief. Running is similar to driving. It's a mind high. While you're running, your mind is elevated. Your endorphins are releasing, your serotonin is boosting. The toxins, the trauma, the pain is leaving your body. Running is my favorite thing in the world.

God speaks clearly to me when I'm running.

I remember one day running on the Prairie Path in Elmhurst, Illinois, on a beautiful sunny day and God spoke to me so clearly. I kept trying to control the situation in my mind. I was having a battle with God. I wouldn't let Arash go, I couldn't. I loved him. I couldn't let the memories go, I couldn't let go of the good times that I was clinging to the bad times and the fear of losing him. That was better than not having Arash at all. I was afraid of a life without Arash. I knew he was going to pass, but I didn't know when. I would wake up each day and painfully think, *Is this the day?*

At this point in the journey, I was hopeless. I was exhausted. I was discouraged. I was drained. I didn't know what else I could do. This was torture. Every day, going to the Perris seeing Arash like this. Only being able to sit with him and watch TV. He couldn't speak, he couldn't walk. This was the man who showed me the world while we were traveling, he held me when my anxiety was at a high, he forgave me for all my mistakes, my flaws, my imperfections. He loved me perfectly. He loved me unconditionally. He loved everyone around him unconditionally.

It was then when I was running I heard God's voice loud and clear. He told me to give up control. & I did. It was all I could do. I was exhausted, drained, lost, hopeless. I couldn't sleep, I couldn't eat, I couldn't take it anymore.

I admitted to myself and to God that God loved Arash more than I did.

Deep breath. Continue on. Keep running.

Chapter 26

Arash Passes, Part 2

The last few days before Arash passed weren't as painful as the weeks prior. After I had listened to this higher power that Arash was loved and he was safe, things got easier for me. It was easier to go over to the Perris, and my perspective changed. I didn't see Arash as in pain or suffering anymore, I saw him in a temporary state waiting. Just waiting.

I can still feel Arash's hand in mine on that final day he passed. I was sitting on his hospital bed next to him in his recliner. His eyes were closed. I held on to his right hand, and in his left hand was the brown rosary that Deacon Mike had given to Arash. Arash held on to this rosary so tightly. He had lost all his strength in his muscles. He had lost weight, his face was thin. He couldn't walk. He couldn't eat. He could barely breathe. But he held on to that rosary with all his strength. All the strength he had, all the life he still had left was used to hold that rosary.

I can still see Arash sitting in that recliner. He is surrounded by family and friends. His face is tinged blue. He is gasping for air as his breathing is rapid and shallow. Like he is swimming up to the top of the ocean gasping for that last breath. But he will achieve that last breath.

The feeling came back. That feeling of having absolutely nothing to cling on to came back. My mistakes, my pain, my wrongdoings, my imperfections flooded my brain. I had no choice but to search into the depths of my soul and face my imperfections, my pain, my mistakes, my wrongs. I looked at everything I did in the dark. You're forced to do this when you have nothing.

"You don't know God is all you need until God is all you got."

Except this time, a different feeling overwhelmed my soul. A feeling of forgiveness, a feeling of thankfulness, a feeling of hope. A feeling of inspiration. A feeling of calmness. The feeling I had when I met Arash for the first time, the feeling I felt when I stepped off that plane in Ireland. The feeling of catching up with an old friend, a feeling of comfort, of safety, of certainty. For the first time in my life, I could see a pathway. A positive pathway. Not one of self-loathing and shame. A path of hope and forgiveness despite what was going on around me. This pathway was as if the greatest, most dependable, reliable, good-hearted, kind, nurturing, loving friend you've ever had was just sitting at the trunk of a tree. Just sitting peacefully. And at a moment's notice, you could just reach your hand out for him and he would be there.

He would be there. From this point on. Always.

I left the Perris house that night with a strange feeling.

Chapter 27

Arash Passes, Part 3

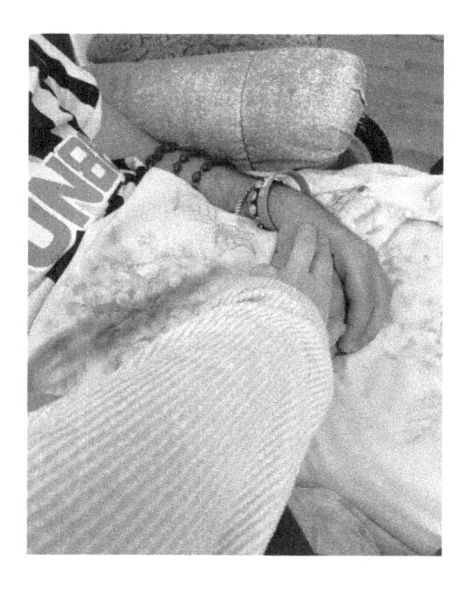

The call. The universal call. The call that is the same in every state and every country. In every culture and every language. That call.

The life-changing call.

"Meg," Arya cries. "Arash passed away."

It was 2am on June 19th, 2022. Father's Day and Juneteenth.

I wake my parents up, and we drive to the Perri's and say good-bye to Arash.

Part 2

Trauma

Chapter 1

Where Do You Go from Here?

I had a lot of time to think after Arash passed away. Taking care of Arash was my main purpose in life for so long. When he passed, I didn't really know what to do. Grief shakes your foundation. It takes the Persian rug you've been standing on for years straight out from under you. The falling is a little painful, you can feel yourself hitting the floor, but after that initial pain, you just sort of float down to a new foundation. And there you are. On a new foundation. Probably one that you've never been on before. Maybe the foundation is sand on a beach, maybe it's concrete in a busy city, maybe it's sticks and rocks in a forest, maybe it's the floor of a new office or the floor of a hospital. Whatever it is, it's new. It's unfamiliar. But there is power in unfamiliarity and change.

Arash passed away in June. The sun came out the next morning, the sun set the next evening. Life moved on. As much as I didn't want it to, life continued to move.

I was surrounded by family and friends during this time. I had emotional support, I had people to lean on, people to listen to me, people whose shoulder I could lean on. I knew I wasn't alone. I knew I had community and support.

But what do you DO? After this?

I had lost my identity. While Arash was sick, my identity was caregiver. Prior to that, my identity was nurse and girlfriend. Prior to that my identity was college student and daughter.

Sure, not all those identities changed after Arash passed. But *I* changed. I didn't know if I wanted to see myself as a caregiver or nurse anymore. Or girlfriend. I felt like I was starting life over again, and to continue on with one of those identities would feel as if I was going backwards.

So I repeated. I clung to what had gotten me through the trauma of what I had just experienced, and I repeated. I repeated the routines that I had done while Arash was sick. I woke up, I ran, I ate healthy. I go to Protein Bar to get a smoothie for Arash…

Wait. Now what?

Do I go back to work? Do I look for a new job? Do I look for a new relationship? Do I make a drastic change? Do I make no change?

What do I DO?

I was lost. Completely and utterly lost. Everyone around me seemed to have an opinion on what I should do. Which I appreciated because I was in no place to turn away any sort of advice, guidance, or love at that time. I didn't know who to listen to or how to move forward. I wasn't sure if I even could move forward.

There it is again. The numbness. It starts to creep into the center of my brain. Consuming my every thought. Altering my brain chemistry. Fogging my sense of self, my sense of identity, my sense of purpose.

×××××

I see a yellow butterfly sitting completely still across the room.

Chapter 2

Nephrology Clinic

Days go by where I am simply going through the motions. I continue to do what I am comfortable with. It makes me feel safe. I don't step out of my comfort zone, I do the exact opposite. I only stay in my comfort zone. I stay with my family, I talk to my friends. I run. I ponder when I should return to work.

I do everything the same. I act the same way I did while Arash was sick. Nothing changes.

I decided to go back to work at the nephrology clinic. The same place where I received the phone call that Arash had a terminal brain tumor on Friday, August 13, the same place where I had to leave when Arash had his first seizure alone at our apartment, the same place where I had leaned on coworkers for comfort and advice during Arash's diagnosis, the same place where I had filed for FMLA months prior. I believe I made this decision to avoid the fear of change. I didn't think I was capable of change. I made a decision to repeat what I had known, what I was comfortable with. I made a decision to align my next move with what society would tell me to do. I took FMLA because my family member was sick, and they are not sick anymore. So the reasonable and rational choice would be to end FMLA and return to work.

So I did. I returned to work in July at the nephrology clinic. I attempted to continue my job right where I left off, thinking this would be a good distraction from the pain and grief I was still feeling.

But something felt off. Coworkers looked at me differently, people that I would normally strike up conversations with avoided talking to me, nobody knew what to say to me. Walking through the hallways seemed narrowing, I could only focus on the wall I leaned against when Arash called me with the horrible news on Friday, August 13. The carpet in the hallways seemed endless. I could only focus on the times I ran on this carpet out of the building when I received medical emergency phone calls from Arash. The lights in the hospital were blinding. I could only focus on the lights at Northwestern when the doctors explained the risks of Arash's upcoming brain surgery. The trauma, the numbness were still consuming the majority of my thoughts.

*****

That yellow butterfly seems to be flying away from me.

Chapter 3

Northwestern Operating Room

I briefly reconnected with an old friend after Arash died. He was working at Northwestern as an anesthesiologist at the time and was dumbfounded when I told him what had happened.

I became inspired again. I remembered how much I loved working in the Operating Room and decided I was going to apply to Northwestern's OR and work in neurosurgery again and change the world. I was inspired to share my story with Northwestern and to use my experience on the other side of patient care as a weapon in strengthening my nursing skills and ultimately strengthening the Northwestern Operating Room Team. I applied for a job in the Operating Room and was called in for an interview almost immediately.

I remember sitting in that interview. I had written in my cover letter about the experience that I had just had with Northwestern and how I was motivated to work for the betterment of neurosurgery after being so personally affected by it. I remember the Operating Room team looking at me with expressions that I couldn't put a name on. They looked at me the way no one has ever looked at me before. I don't know if it was confusion or disbelief or inspiration or sympathy or what. The interviewers explained to me that all new nurses hired to the peri-operative team typically rotate through each specialty, and then the surgery specialty teams (ENT, orthopedics, cardiovascular, spine, etc.) see which nurses fit best with their team, and ultimately, they pair them up based on a sort of matching system. They explained to me that since I had previous surgery experience working as part of the neuro/spine team for two years at Elmhurst, they were going to hire me to the spine team immediately, which is something they had never done before. They hired me shortly after.

*****

The yellow butterfly sits perfectly still.

*****

I started working in the operating room in August 2022, a month and a half after Arash had passed away. At first, it was great. It was a great distraction, and all the things that I loved about the Operating Room—the fast pace, the high stakes, the big egos, the patient advocation—were brought to the forefront of my mind. The trauma and numbness feelings were pushed to the back of my brain. I loved going to work. I moved into an apartment in Streeterville, Chicago, with my best friend, Emily. I was a five-minute walk to and from the hospital. I was the first person on the spine team to work every day, and I would volunteer to stay late if needed. I was eager to learn. I went to team happy hours and tried my best to mingle with the team.

*****

Northwestern had high expectations. They are the ninth best hospital in the nation. Coming in with two years of spine experience and being the first RN to be hired to the spine team immediately raised the bar even higher.

I was matched with a preceptor, and he would be my instructor to train me both in being a scrub nurse, where you are actively scrubbed into surgery handling sterile surgical instruments and handing them to the surgeon and when you are circulating when you are unsterile and are not scrubbed into the actual surgery. The nurse is charting and calling for items that the patient or surgery team needs during the surgery, among many other things.

*****

I began as a scrub nurse first. I had no previous experience scrubbing before, only circulating. I can honestly say I did my absolute best to keep up with the surgeries, learn the instruments, learn surgeon preferences, keep counts accurate, keep organization, and keep a positive attitude.

One of the doctors had a reputation for being the "hot" doctor on the spine team. He was young, handsome, and played fun music in the OR. Most nurses preferred to be in his surgeries. My third time scrubbing in one of his cases, the doctor makes a comment to me at the beginning of the case. "Wow, Megan, you're becoming quite the pro." My preceptor, who at this point has been letting me scrub cases slightly more independently in attempts to only be used as a reference, stepped into the surgery and began to grill me. He critiqued everything I was doing to a degree of perfection that he had never done before. At the end of the case, the resident physician even joked at my preceptor, "Jeez!"

I was up for the challenge, but something didn't sit quite right with me about this. My relationship with my preceptor changed this day.

*****

The yellow butterfly is flying into fog. I can only barely see it.

I am scrubbing in another case. This time with a different doctor. One of the most important things in surgery is making sure everything stays sterile so that no bacteria is present on surgical instruments to avoid the patient getting an infection. I am scrubbing in a spine case, and I notice the resident physician had a hole in one of his gloves. I alerted the physician as soon as I noticed it and asked him to change his gloves. My preceptor stepped in. "Megan, you shouldn't tell the doctor that if they're in the middle of something else." The resident physician said, "Thanks for the heads-up," and switched his gloves.

I was confused. Isn't the whole point of keeping everything sterile to avoid infection for the patient? If the doctor has a hole in his glove, that is the closest place where bacteria could enter the patient's body? Something still didn't sit right with me.

*****

The clinical educator pulls me out of the room that I'm circulating in one day and informs me that the spine team has told her that I am not doing well, I am not advancing at the pace that they would expect, and that I need to step up my game.

The numbness comes back. Suddenly, all I can focus on are the bright lights of the OR, and I'm transported to the Northwestern hallway where I once sat with Arash's family, and I am now walking down the hall as an employee now. The numbness lingers.

I am confused. Nothing bad has happened. Sure, I've made minor mistakes, but I started this job only weeks ago. You do not learn the operating room in a few weeks, it takes time to truly feel comfortable in a new OR. No patient has been injured, no surgeries turned emergent, no surgeon had yelled at me for doing something wrong (which in my previous experience, I know would be the case if I truly was doing a bad job). I was so confused. None of the nurses had said anything to me about how I wasn't doing well. Or how I wasn't progressing accordingly.

I am angry. I return to the operating room and can't help but tell my preceptor what the educator said. I asked him, "Do you truly think I'm doing a bad job?" He didn't answer right way. He just said, "Prove them wrong."

Something still just doesn't sit right with me.

A memory resurfaces. On the very first day I started at Northwestern, I had a different female preceptor who was later on assigned to be my mentor. I asked my preceptor where pre-op was because this was my first day and I hadn't been there to get a patient yet. I found out later on that she had reported this to the clinical educator, saying, "It doesn't seem like Megan has the experience that she says she does."

*****

Grief has a way of morphing your reality. Looking back on it, I'm sure there was some truth to the criticisms of my work performance at the time.

*****

Two weeks pass, and I am called into the office again. The clinical instructor, the team manager, and I sit at a long brown table, all in chairs that are extremely far apart from each other. This time, it is a formal meeting to discuss how I am being placed on a work improvement plan and if I didn't improve my work performance I would be terminated in two weeks. Neither of these instructors has seen me do absolutely anything in the operating room; they are basing this meeting completely on what other nurses have reported to them about my performance.

The numbness comes back to my brain. This time, it is completely overwhelming. This time, the numbness actually travels from my brain to my body. I am transported to sitting in the doctor's office where Arash's neurologist first pulled up his horrible MRI. The lights in the office begin to become blinding. They are so blinding it's like I actually cannot see. I'm transported to watching the surgery team wheel Arash back for surgery. I am transported to having a discussion regarding Arash's care while he wasn't even in the room. I am swimming to the surface gasping for that last breath of air.

*****

The yellow butterfly is gone. Completely and utterly gone.

*****

This meeting occurred on a Friday, and I sat with this news all weekend. I was so upset, I was so angry. The ninth best hospital in the world who couldn't save Arash is telling me that I'm not good enough? I was furious.

I called my brother Brendan first and asked his advice.

Brendan is my younger brother but has always felt like my older brother. He is protective and dependable. He is honest and trustworthy. He is often my first call in a crisis. Brendan was dealing with some health issues at this time and was also seeing Northwestern for answers but wasn't having much luck with getting answers or treatment. I explained to Brendan how what was going on in the OR was contradicting everything that my educator and manager were telling me. I explained that there is no way I could be doing bad enough to get fired. Nothing bad had happened, no patient was injured, no surgery had gone wrong. I was in training, and I wasn't perfect, but there is no way I could be doing this bad.

Brendan, being the supportive brother that he was, told me, "Meg, if you stay there, you're going to lose your mind."

I still sat with this all weekend. Not sure of the right course of action. At this point, the numbness was constant. It was at the forefront of my brain. It was my main focus. It clouded my thoughts as I'm sure it clouded my judgment.

*****

I walk into work on Monday and go to look at my assignment. I was still on training and was typically matched up with a preceptor. I walk up to the spine board assignment and look down. My assignment on the sheet of paper states that I am scrubbing with a preceptor and another nurse is circulating. Except this is crossed out with a pencil and it says that I am circulating on my own without a preceptor and there is only one scrub nurse.

My mind explodes. I don't think I've ever been this mad before in my life. How could I be assigned to be on my own in a neurosurgery case at the ninth best hospital in the world if I am doing bad enough to be on the verge of termination?

The numbness now turns a fiery red and engulfs my entire brain and entire body. God is screaming to me in this moment.

I march back to the operating room and tell the team I am done. I have my exit interview in the manager's office very soon after, and I leave Northwestern. That was my last day.

*****

The yellow butterfly starts to return. I can only see a peek of it in the clouds.

Chapter 4

Reflections from a Balcony

All we got is memories, so what the f——ck is time.

—Mac Miller, "Thoughts from a Balcony"

Grief has a way of making you feel completely alone. You can be surrounded by people every second of every day and still feel completely alone. Like no one understands what you're going through. Even though everyone around me in my family and Arash's family had also just gone through a year of a very traumatic experience just as I did, I still feel like they couldn't relate to what I personally was going through. I had lost my love. I had lost my best friend. I was in the most pain. I, I, I…

It's hard not to be selfish when you're grieving. It's like you come face-to-face with your ego and have no choice but to constantly talk to it, constantly evaluate it, and constantly entertain it.

I remember that intense feeling of being alone like it was yesterday. Like at a moment's notice, I could call up my old friend loneliness for the night and he would come over. And I could sit with him all night. And let him dominate me. That is how close I was to that feeling during my final days at Northwestern. I was going through the motions of life, but I was completely alone. I would go to work and be surrounded by people in the OR, but I was still alone. I would come home from work and spend time with my family and friends, but I was still alone. I would continue to go through the motions, wake up, go to a job that I couldn't depend on anymore, come home, worry about going to that same job the next day, and sit with my numbness and loneliness for the night. This continued for many nights. Many, many nights. I would go out in Chicago and spend time with friends and return just to my apartment, and that loneliness was still waiting for me. I would spend time with my family, but when I arrived back to my apartment, that loneliness was still waiting for me. I would go on a run and return, and that loneliness was still waiting for me. Every single night. Nothing could shake it. It was my new norm.

But when I listened to that higher power when I arrived to work that Monday and saw my assignment for the day, I can confidently say this was a turning point for me. I left Northwestern, and I felt free. The chains of trying to prove myself to others, the chains of living for how I thought I should be living, the chains of returning to a cycle of familiarity that clearly wasn't working for me, the chains slightly began to release. I had lost a sense of control in that moment, but I wasn't afraid. I felt empowered.

After I left Northwestern, I took a walk alongside the Lakefront Path on Lake Michigan in Chicago. A feeling of forgiveness and freedom overwhelmed me. I also remember this feeling like it was yesterday. Like at a moment's notice I could also call up an old friend freedom for the night and he could come over. And I could sit with him all night and let him dominate me. I walked for a long time that day and took in what I had just done. Actually, I took in what I had just listened to do.

"Am I crazy?" was my initial thought. I had never walked out on a job before in my life. I actually have had multiple jobs in my life and did well. I was a hard worker, I never called out sick, I always made work a priority. When I worked in the Elmhurst OR, I did very well, and was even awarded for excellent achievement in the OR for my work as a circulating nurse during a life-threatening case. Work as a nurse had always been my identity, and I realized in that moment walking by the lake that I had just made a decision that completely contradicted my identity. I had lost control. As the world would see it, I made an irrational, impulsive decision, and for that, I should be anxious, concerned, and afraid. I had just lost a part of myself that I had clung on to for so long. I am a nurse.

Not anymore. At least, not for a little while.

*****

The yellow butterfly continues to peek through the clouds and fog.

*****

Looking back on it, I am making peace with the troubling time I had at Northwestern. I was mad at them still, and my reality was morphed. One of the critiques that was given by my peers was that "I seemed distracted" in the OR. This was true. They were right. I was distracted. Was this safe for an OR nurse to be distracted in the OR? No. I am coming to terms with the trauma that I endured. This trauma morphed my perspective for so long. When my peers offered constructive feedback to my clinical instructor, my first instinct was to protect my ego. It was fragile. When in reality, the Megan prior to this experience would trust this feedback and work to improve my performance. The Megan before this would cling to these comments and let it define her and consume her thoughts. These comments would keep her up all night. They would control her. The approval of others. It used to be my biggest motivator. I think it's a lot of people's biggest motivator. Humankind is made for community. It's why the worst prison sentence is solitary confinement. It's why quarantining for COVID was so horrible. I don't think it's bad to value the opinions of others and take in account constructive feedback, but when the approval for others becomes the biggest, most controlling thought in your brain, you're in trouble.

I knew I was.

Many nights when I worked in the OR at Elmhurst, I was restless. I couldn't sleep nights before cases because I was afraid of making mistakes the next day, I was afraid of what people would think about me. I had many friends in the OR, and most surgeons loved to work with me. However, this was a result of my intense need to please people. I would bend over backwards to make sure that people saw me in a way I wanted them to. It wasn't authentic. I only wanted to go to work and have a day where no one said anything mean to me, nobody hurt my feelings, nothing bad happened, and I could go home feeling safe.

Phew. Another day done. Another day of the surgeon thanking me at the end of a surgery and not screaming at me. No huge problems. Phew.

Arash did not live this way. He did not care what other people thought about him. It was endearing, it was refreshing, it was probably my favorite thing about him. Many nights, especially during the COVID-19 pandemic, Arash held me as my anxiety skyrocketed anticipating the unknown at work the next day. Arash was my rock. He was strong. He was encouraging. He told me, "You got this," and he would remind me that it doesn't matter what people think. Go in to work, do the best for your patient, and come home.

I am so thankful for his perspective on life. I am so thankful for the nights where Arash listened to me cry and worry during the COVID-19 pandemic. I was not easy to be around working as a nurse during the pandemic. I was afraid all the time. I was worried all the time. He stuck with me, though. Through everything. He loved me despite my fears, despite my insecurities, my imperfections.

*****

When I look back at my time at the nephrology clinic and my time at the Northwestern OR after Arash passed, I am starting to see it. I was suffering from the trauma. It was affecting my functioning. My reactions were heightened, I was extremely paranoid, and I was isolating myself socially. I could not control the unwanted memories, and they were consuming me. I was anxious and depressed. And I could no longer hide it, people were noticing.

I'm sure this affected my ability to perform my job at the same level that I did in the Elmhurst OR.

The numbness was everywhere. The loneliness was overwhelming. I had changed, but I was continuing to cling to old habits. Both jobs that I had taken after Arash passed were jobs that I had already performed. It wasn't new. I was clinging to what was routine, what was comfortable. But what do you do when even those routines begin to become uncomfortable? I was comfortable working in the nephrology clinic, but now when I went back to work, all I could see were the unwanted memories of past trauma that occurred while I was there. I was comfortable working in the operating room, but now I was distracted and didn't see things the same way as the people in the operating room did. Things that didn't seem important to me were extremely important to them. I had changed.

I couldn't tell if the nurse who used to be able to perform at a high level in neurosurgery no longer could or if she no longer *wanted* to.

The trauma, the numbness, the pain were at the center of my brain. Constantly.

I think we all suffer from trauma to some degree. I think it's universal. I sincerely think that the pain and suffering we all feel at times is universal. I don't think any person's brain is completely absent of trauma. Different backgrounds, different upbringings, different life events, and genetics play a role in this level of trauma. But it's present for everyone. I think everyone has different triggers that make this trauma come to the front of their mind.

And I don't think it's beneficial to avoid this trauma from never being at the fore center of your brain. I think we can use this trauma to change for the better. Maybe we can morph our brain mechanisms to see the trauma in a different way. In a way, that allows us to continue on.

*****

Flashback 1: *American Honey*

The first movie Arash and I watched together was *American Honey*, a beautiful film about an adolescent girl from a troubled home who runs away to drive across the American Midwest selling magazine subscriptions door-to-door with a gang of teenagers, one of whom is Jake (Shia LaBeouf). She soon gets into the group's lifestyle of hard-partying nights, law-bending days, and young love.

I'm instantly transported to Arash's first apartment. We are madly in love. We had just met and can't keep our hands off each other. I'm lying on his gray L-shaped couch wearing a warm fuzzy sweater as the fall temperatures in Chicago are beginning to slightly drop. The crispy slight draft from the window next to me is sending a chill down my spine. Goose bumps line my thighs and my arms. The soft hair on my arms is standing up. Arash is walking to the couch from his bedroom with a warm down comforter. A wave of relief overwhelms my body.

"Don't start it yet!" says Arash.

> There's a wild, wild whisper
> Blowing in the wind
> Calling out my name like a long lost friend
> Oh I miss those days as the years go by
> Oh nothing's sweeter than summertime
> And American honey
> Get caught in the race
> Of this crazy life
> Trying to be everything can make you lose your
> mind
> I just wanna go back in time
> To American honey, yeah.
> (Lady Antebellum, "American Honey")

Arash is lying behind me on the couch. His breath is whispering on my neck. His breath is steady. It's unchanging. The warmth of his breath starts to settle the goose bumps on my skin. His warm hand holds my cold fingertips with the strength of that tension in his body. I adjust my hand; he does not let it go. His heart beats against my back. I can feel it through my thick sweater. The warmth of his heart sends a lasting warmth through my bloodstream.

The warmth's not going anywhere.

Flashback 2: Union Pier, Michigan

Arash and I are driving up to Union Pier, Michigan, to go on a weekend summer getaway with my family. The sun is shining, the windows are down, the breeze is blowing through our hair. Arash grabs my hand as he drives and moves his black Ray-Ban sunglasses from his forehead to his eyes and turns up the stereo.

Once we arrive, we pack a cooler and make our way to the beach to meet my family. My mom is sitting on a long pink beach towel, sipping on a Bud Light Lime. My sister, Shannon, is sitting next to her in her black bikini, fiddling with the speaker. My dad and my brothers, Sean and Brendan, are wearing their swim trunks and throwing a football back and forth, alternating with breaks for a beer. Arash and I take our flip-flops off, and our toes sink into the warm sand. The sun hits our skin, and the sun is rejuvenating our souls.

"You made it!"

Shannon turns up the volume of the stereo.

> So it's hard to find
> Someone with that kind of intensity
> You touched my hand, I played it cool
> And you reached out your hand to me
> But if our paths never cross
> Well, no, I'm not sorry, but
> If I live to see the seven wonders
> I'll make a path to the rainbow's end
> I'll never live to match the beauty again
> The rainbow's edge
> (Fleetwood Mac, "Seven Wonders")

Arash runs into the ocean as the sun is setting and grabs my hand.

*****

My family, Arash, and I return to the backyard of the summer-house, the bonfire is crackling, the flames are warming our skin, the beers are warming our blood. The music is warming our souls. We are dancing and laughing. Yellow butterflies are fluttering around the bonfire.

Chapter 5

Lakefront Path

As I mentioned, after I left Northwestern, my first move was to immediately take a walk along the Chicago Lakefront path. This path is five minutes from Northwestern, and I had my AirPods in and was honestly just trying to decompress, catch my breath, slow my heart rate, and get my feet back on the ground. It was a chilly November day, but I remember taking the longest walk of my life that day. I really was just listening for guidance, for direction. I didn't have much going on in my head. I hadn't told anyone that I had just quit my job at this point. I was just existing and walking. That's really all there was to it.

The numbness. I guess that's kind of the definition of numbness? I had nothing going on in my head. I had no thoughts, no opinions, no ideas, no leads, no direction. That numbness, here it is again, at the forefront of my brain. But it was different this time.

I was walking next to the lake. The waves were crashing against the shore. Over & over. Runners and bikers were passing me by as I walked along the path. Nobody was looking at me. Nobody was focused on me. Nobody knew me. A feeling of relief overwhelmed my body.

To my left I see the beautifully designed skyscrapers lining Lake Shore Drive. I see the cars cruising down Lake Shore Drive. I see Northwestern's campus. And to the right there is Lake Michigan. The waves of the lake crash and crash. Again & again.

My mind is transported to sitting at Arash's house with him during one of the last days of his life. I am sitting on his hospital bed while he is sitting in his recliner to the left of me. He cannot talk, he cannot walk, he cannot speak. But in his left hand, he is holding Deacon Mike's rosary as tight as he used to hold my hand. I am holding his right hand, & in front of me, I see a pathway. Not a traumatic pathway. A peaceful pathway. To the left of me is my absolute worst nightmare. My dear Arash is dying. He is gasping for air. But when I looked forward, a sense of relief overwhelms my body because I think Arash and me in that moment saw the same peaceful pathway, that same peaceful friend.

*****

Old people-pleasing Megan starts to resurface: "What will people think about you?" "What are you going to tell people?" "Are you even a nurse anymore?" "Who do you think you are?" But this time, as these thoughts try to come to the center of my mind, I made a conscious decision to slowly push these thoughts away. I am swimming to the surface of the ocean, and these thoughts are trying to drag me down, but I made a conscious decision to kick them down.

I made a decision to focus on the beauty of the seemingly infinite and beautiful Lake Michigan on my right. Not to focus on the skyscrapers, the cars, or Northwestern's campus next to me on my left.

I made a choice to listen to the power that told me in that moment to leave Northwestern. And I was going to follow that power from now on.

*****

Arash chuckles and takes a sip of his favorite energy drink. "Jeez, Meg, you really think you're a philosopher over here."

A yellow butterfly lands on his head.

Flashback 3

It's a Friday night. Arash and I just popped open a special bottle of champagne that was gifted to us at our housewarming party. We are taking turns putting songs on the speaker queue. We are dancing together. Yellow butterflies everywhere.

> Hear me now!
> I'm down on knees and praying
> Though my faith is weak
> Without you so please, baby, please
> Give us a chance
> Make amends and I will stand up 'til the end
> A million times, a trillion more
> (Empire of the Sun and Mac Miller, "The Spins")

I'm looking into Arash's beautiful brown eyes while we are holding hands, dancing.

Flashback 4

We are in my cozy studio apartment just days after Arash and I had gone on our first date. We are making pancakes in my tiny kitchen with the Newcastle United soccer game on TV in the background. I'm sitting on the kitchen counter, and Arash is standing in front of me, giving me a long hug. I try to break free, but he won't let go.

"Arash! The pancakes are starting to burn!" I laugh.

*****

Flashback 5

When Arash was back at home on hospice care, my grandma gave Arash a gift. It was a stone that had the Irish blessing on it:

> May the road rise to meet you. May the wind always be at your back. May the sun shine warm upon your face & rains fall soft upon your fields. May God hold you in the palm of His hands.

Chapter 6

Misericordia

AN IRISH BLESSING

May the road rise up
to meet you. May the wind be
always at your back.
May the sun shine warm upon
your face; the rains fall soft
upon your fields and until we
meet again, may God hold you
in the palm of His hand.

45.

I reconnected with an old friend. He truly couldn't have been kinder to me in the darkest days of my life. I still think about him often.

I was inspired again.

I'm going to go work for a nonprofit organization. I'm going to use my experience to help those in need and change the world.

Misericordia Home is a beautiful place in Chicago, Illinois. It is an assisted-living facility for people that have intellectual and developmental disabilities. It's a Catholic organization, and I had heard about it through church. The organization was started in 1921 and began as a maternity hospital for women of meager means, both married and unwed, at 2916 West Forty-Seventh Street in Chicago. A little more than thirty years later in 1954, Misericordia recognized an even-greater need in society—helping young children with intellectual, developmental, and physical disabilities (misericordiahome. com).

It is currently run by Sister Rosemary Connelly. She is a beautiful, kind eighty-nine-year-old woman who has done so much in her life to help others and give a home to society's most underserved.

Misericordia's campus contains many different facilities that home their residents; these groupings are based on the severity of their special needs. The organization hires nurses who pass medications, complete assessments, coordinate doctor's appointments, coordinate dental appointments, etc. The nurses typically work as case managers for the residents.

When family members can no longer provide the care that the residents need at their homes, they can call Misericordia to be put on a wait list to have their loved one moved into the facility so they can receive optimal care for their special needs. Typically, families move their residents in when they are aging and can no longer physically provide care to their loved ones.

It truly is a special place.

Both the staff members and volunteers work tirelessly to not only provide care to these residents but also to enrich the quality of their lives. The organization holds "day training programs" daily for residents to keep their cognitive skills at optimal performance. They participate in activities daily with other residents to promote community. Employees and volunteers take the residents on field trips around the community to experience the joys of the world. Misericordia is home to the most delicious bakery you will ever try. The residents work at this bakery, enriching their daily life and sense of purpose.

The residents at Misericordia are truly some of the most joyful people I have ever met.

They have every reason to be angry and bitter because of their disability, but they couldn't be further from that. They are kind, joyful, happy, friendly, welcoming, and faithful. They are truly an inspiration.

*****

I began working at Misericordia in January 2023. I thoroughly enjoyed my time there. I started off as a nurse and was trained to work in the Rosemary-Connelly facility. There, I would pass seizure medications to residents, complete assessments, help with ADLs (activities of daily living), help coordinate care between physicians, and communicate with families on the status of their loved ones.

The Rosemary-Connelly facility homed residents with moderate to severe disabilities. All the residents in this facility were in wheelchairs and had little mobility. Some residents could speak, but most were nonverbal. This didn't stop the residents from smiling every day as they attended day training programs and field trips.

*****

The yellow butterflies multiply.

*****

I enjoyed going to work every day. My coworkers were great. The work was fulfilling. And I felt like I had a purpose again. Misericordia is a special place, and I felt blessed to have had the opportunity to work there.

Time passes, and within a few months, I encountered my first extreme challenge at Misericordia.

I had been floated to a different facility, the Marian Center, because the nursing need was greater there than at Rosemary-Connelly that day. I had been trained in this facility, but I hadn't been back to it for a while, and I felt a little uneasy because I was out of my comfort zone. I had grown accustomed to working at the

Rosemary-Connelly Home. I knew the residents, I knew their needs, and floating to a different facility had put me on edge.

The residents in the Marian Center were severely disabled and could have behavioral episodes of agitation from time to time. As anyone could.

I am in the nursing office when I get a phone call from one of the staff members working in the Marian Center that a resident had shown physical aggression toward another resident.

My heart rate starts to increase, my palms start to sweat, my senses begin to heighten. Anxiety and fear increase in my brain, consuming my thoughts.

I leave the nurses' office and go to the Marian Center to check on the resident. The resident's hand is bleeding profusely. Red blood is pouring from his hand down his wheelchair to the floor.

The trauma returns. The trauma floods my brain. The red blood brings my mind back to the night Arash awakened in a tonic-clonic seizure. The redness of the blood brings me back to red flashing lights of the sirens on the ambulance illuminating our bedroom. The sirens are loud and piercing my eardrums. The trauma returns to my brain. My heart rate increases, my breath increases, my palms sweat. The images are repeating over and over again. I am existing and waiting for the EMT to arrive.

I enter fight-or-flight mode. I stop the bleeding of the resident's hand by applying pressure. I sit with the resident as he begins to calm down. As I hold the gauze as pressure on his hand, I can feel his body begin to stop shaking. I begin to feel my heart rate decreasing. Once the bleeding stops, I apply a dressing to the resident's hand and sit with him until he begins to return back to himself.

Phew.

*****

The other yellow butterflies leave; there's only one yellow butterfly in sight. And it's fluttering away.

*****

The next day at work, I get a call into the manager's office. "Megan, we are concerned with how you handled that situation yesterday. A supervisor should have been notified, an incident report should have been completed."

The numbness returns. My vision begins to blur, my hearing starts to deafen. I cannot feel my legs. I don't know what to say, I don't know what to do. I am existing. Purely existing. No thoughts are in my brain. Just numbness.

I needed help.

I felt exposed. I could no longer hide this trauma. The trauma was pouring out of me. It had overtaken me. It had morphed my perspective. It had morphed my judgment. It had morphed my reality. This trauma was now affecting others negatively. I needed help.

I vividly remember walking down the hallway after that meeting. The hallway was long, and the walls were white. It seemed to go on for eternity. The lights were bright and blinding. I felt weak in my legs. I felt like they could no longer support me.

Trauma had engulfed me.

*****

The yellow butterfly is gone.

*****

I made an appointment to see a psychiatrist shortly after this happened. I had shared what had happened with my family, and they encouraged me to seek help. So I did.

I met with a psychiatrist and explained everything to her. From the beginning. I told her about Arash, I told her about Northwestern and the most recent incident at Misericordia.

Diagnosis: post-traumatic stress disorder (PTSD).

Definition: a disorder in which a person has difficulty recovering after experiencing or witnessing a terrifying event.

The condition may last months or years, with triggers that can bring back memories of the trauma accompanied by intense emotional and physical reactions. Symptoms may include nightmares or unwanted memories of the trauma, avoidance of situations that bring back memories of the trauma, heightened reactions, anxiety, or a depressed mood.

A wave of relief overwhelms me. Okay, there is a name to this feeling. This is a real thing. There was something wrong. I felt hopeful. Okay, the problem is identified. There are solutions to this problem. Now I can work to fix the problem.

*****

> If God exists, it shouldn't be a problem.
> (Post Malone, "Socialite")

*****

Chicago Marathon Grant Park

Chicago Marathon 2024: starting line.

I am standing in a sea of runners. Next to me is my sister and best friend, Shannon. We are pacing back and forth to keep our muscles warm. We are wearing sweatshirts and sweatpants, and the crisp air of a fall Chicago marathon is sending a chill through our bones. I have never felt this type of adrenaline before. I am up for the challenge. I am ready to go. I completed the training; I can do this. I am about to run a marathon.

*****

I think PTSD is universal. When I think of PTSD, I think of war veterans who have witnessed horrible, horrible things overseas. And I think of a disconnect. There's no way I have PTSD. I didn't go to war. But what is war? Is war limited to just the actual physical act of serving in a war? Is it only identified as serving in the military, marines, or Navy? Or enlisting in the army for the freedom of our country?

I don't think so. I think every person has their own war going on inside them. Whether that be a war against greed, envy, desire, violence, anger, lust, etc. I think that this internal war in each and every one of us can cause PTSD. The scale of trauma differs from person to person. It differs in severity. The presence of this trauma in your brain comes in waves. At some points in life, that trauma causes a disorder. And at some points in life, you're the war hero. It's a continuous war.

> I say love
> Don't mean nothing
> 'Less there's something
> Worth fighting for
> It's a beautiful War
> (Kings of Leon, "Beautiful War")

Flashback 4

Arash and I's first trip together was in New Orleans, Louisiana.

We are sitting on a small blue boat with a tour guide and a few other passengers. We are cruising through a bayou to explore a swamp in New Orleans. The boat is moving at a slow, reasonable pace, making you feel at ease. Small drops of water from the swamp are splashing and sprinkling into the boat, keeping you alert. The sun is shining. There are three large alligators to your left. They are moving slowly in the swamp and peeking their heads up above the water. The tour guide assures you that you are safe. These alligators do not want to hurt us. The wind blows through our hair, and for a single minute, we have reached the ultimate level of happiness.

A yellow butterfly lands at the front of the boat.

> Now tell me how you love it.
> You know you at the top when only heaven is
> right above it.
> (Lil Wayne, "Right Above It")

Chapter 7

Panic

 Los Angeles, California

Things begin to get better. After seeing the psychiatrist and accepting my diagnosis, I begin to work on healing. I prioritize my health and continue to spend time with my friends and family.

Things are looking better. The trauma fades to the back of my mind, and I am in a good mental place. I can focus on my job again. I feel more energized. The loneliness and pain are still present, but not as much.

If I call up my old friend loneliness for the night, there's a chance he can't make it.

So I'll call up my old friend freedom instead.

I begin to do better at work. I'm feeling more confident in my abilities. I forgive myself for the previous incident as now I can confidently say that the root cause of this problem was the avoidance factor of my PTSD.

I can honestly look at myself in the mirror and know that I did not mean harm. I was avoiding any situation that had reminded me of the past trauma. It was a symptom of my PTSD.

I felt like I had gained control again of my life, of my thoughts, of my future.

There was a new job position opening at Misericordia. It was to be the nurse at one of the facilities, ironically named the Shannon Apartments. The Shannon Apartments were home to the highest-functioning residents at Misericordia. These residents could walk and were verbal. They worked jobs on the campus. There were fifty residents in the building, and the nurse's job was to advocate for their care by completing assessments, scheduling appointments, following up with specialists, ensuring the residents had their medications every month, and so on.

The residents at Shannon Apartments are delightful. They are kind, friendly, social, and hardworking. They have weekly happy hours, weekly karaoke dance parties and have cultivated the sincerest friendships with one another. It's a happy and joyful place to be.

I was feeling inspired and up for the challenge of more responsibility as a nurse at Misericordia, so I applied for the position of the Shannon Apartments nurse. I got the position and started this new job in September of 2023.

*****

Things are still going well. I am excited for the new position. I am excited for more responsibility and to grow my career at Misericordia. The past two nurses who worked in this role at Shannon Apartments had moved on to become the directors of nursing at Misericordia. I was inspired and excited. Things were going well.

*****

I face my first major challenge at the Shannon Apartments.

At Misericordia, when there is an emergency on campus, a "Nurse Report" is called. This is when reception will call a "Nurse Report" over the intercom system, sort of like a "Code Blue" in the hospital. This is usually called for a variety of reasons: a resident has fallen or a resident is having a seizure or another medical emergency. A nurse report really could mean anything.

I am sitting in the nursing office at Shannon Apartments, and a nurse report is called over the intercom at Rosemary-Connelly Home, the place that I used to work. I run over to the Rosemary-Connelly Home as one of the residents is having a seizure that will not stop. All the nurses are present, and one of them tending to the resident at the time looks up and yells, "Somebody call 911!"

I run to the supervisor's office to grab the phone and call 911, and the EMT on the other line begins to ask question about the resident, and I realize in that moment that I don't know the answers. I wasn't familiar with the situation at hand. I didn't know how long the resident was having a seizure, I didn't know their vital signs, I didn't know what kind of care was being provided across the room as I was on the phone in the supervisor's office.

My mind freezes. The numbness. It's back. It had been gone for so long at this point. The trauma. It's back. In a flash, my mind is transported to Arash's seizure in the middle of the night. My mind is then transferred to the lasting seizure he had on hospice care at his home in Algonquin. We called 911, and I rode with Arash in the ambulance to the hospital. My mind is numb, it's gone. It left.

The yellow butterfly is gone. Again!

"Ma'am?" the EMT asks me over the phone.

I go into fight-or-flight mode again. I blacked out as I did when I was speaking at Arash's funeral when I was reading from the paper in front of me surrounded by a sea of blackness. I don't remember exactly what I said to the EMT over the phone, I just told them to come to Misericordia. I panicked. I don't know what I said. I know it wasn't accurate. That trauma was back. The trauma that I had gone months successfully avoiding was back. I look at the resident having a seizure, and I see Arash. My nursing mind shuts off. And I enter survival mode.

The EMTs burst through the doors of Misericordia and run to the resident.

"Who called 911?" one of the EMTs ask.

That's when it happened. My first panic attack.

My heart rate skyrockets. My heart is beating so fast I feel as if my heart is going to burst through my scrubs. My breath becomes shallow. I begin to gasp for air. It takes all my strength to keep breathing. I can see Arash gasping for those last breaths. I cannot feel my legs. They cannot support my weight any longer. I am swimming to the top of that ocean; I am so close to the top. I am breaths away from it.

Deep breath. Deep breath. Remember the pathway.

Breathe. Breathe. Breathe.

Fight-or-flight mode increases. I need to escape. I need to leave. I can't watch this. I can't see this. I can't answer the EMT. I can't be a nurse. I can't.

"Megan, are you okay?" one of the nurses asks.

"Uh…yeah," I lie.

I turn around and leave Rosemary-Connelly through the exit doors at the back of the building. I cannot breathe. I am breathing so rapidly. My body is clinging to every particle of air it can grasp. My legs are about to give out. I have lost control. I am going to die. I cannot breathe. The trauma. It's overwhelming. It has completely dominated me. Where do I go? What do I do?

Breathe. Breathe. Breathe.

This lasts for fifteen minutes. In my mind, it lasted for eternity.

I made it back to Shannon Apartments. Sister Rosemary Connelly lives in an apartment at this facility.

I didn't know where to go. I didn't know what to do. I was lost in the infinite ocean.

I knock on Sister Rosemary's door.

"Come in."

*****

I had only met Sister Rosemary once prior to this moment. COVID-19 was running rapidly through the Shannon Apartments a few weeks prior, and I was asked to do a nasal COVID test on her. It was negative.

*****

"Hi, Sister Rosemary," I panted. "Can I sit here for a while?"

"Of course, my dear!"

I sit on her green comfy couch. Her apartment is covered in trinkets and crosses. It is warm. Her couch is covered with blankets. Eighty-nine-year-old Sister Rosemary is sitting in her recliner, reading the newspaper. She has a warmth and welcoming presence. It feels as if you are sitting at your late grandmother's house.

"Honey, what's wrong?"

I catch my breath and explain what had just happened. "I'm sorry, Sister Rosemary. I think I'm having a panic attack, and I didn't know where to go."

A look of loving concern fills her face. "The Lord brought you here, honey."

I explain to her that I don't know why I jumped into this situation. I told her about Arash and how this had just triggered a panic attack and I was afraid that this was going to negatively affect the resident.

She told me to learn from this and move forward.

*****

The resident had a heart attack but received care in the hospital and returned safely back to Misericordia.

*****

When the silence isn't quiet
And it feels like it's getting hard to breathe
And I know you feel like dying
But I promise we'll take the world to its feet
And move mountains
Bring it to its feet
And move mountains
And I'll rise up
I'll rise like the day
I'll rise up
I'll rise unafraid
I'll rise up
And I'll do it a thousand times again
(Andria Day, "Rise Up")

Flashback 5

Arash and I are in Ireland. We are on a bus tour that is traveling through the Irish countryside. To my left are green pastures, and to my right are green pastures. These extend across the country for as far as I can see. The tour guide is speaking in her Irish brogue with her Irish wit. I look to my left, and Arash is sitting next to me with his head against the window of the bus. He is sleeping peacefully. Behind him, images of perfect green pastures go on & on.

These images are everlasting.

A yellow butterfly lands on the window outside.

*****

I held the wise words of Sister Rosemary close to my heart.

arash12
New Orleans, Louisiana
...

Chapter 8

Going Backwards? Part 1

After this panic attack, I was alarmed. I had never experienced this type of physical discomfort. I was coming to terms with the trauma that occurred in my mind, but now I realized I could not restrict this trauma only to my brain anymore; it had poured from my brain to my body once again. I had just experienced an episode where I truly thought I was going to die for fifteen minutes. I was concerned. And scared. I was afraid of another panic attack occurring.

I returned to my apartment after work that day.

I'll go ahead and call loneliness up tonight.

*****

Chicago Marathon 2024: mile 5.

I am running. The crisp, cold air of a fall Chicago day is still chilling my skin. The initial excited adrenaline of the race slowly begins to wear off, and reality starts to sink in. You have twenty-one more miles to go. Listen to the music and find inspiration. Look at the crowd and find inspiration. Read the signs and find inspiration. You have trained for this. You can do this. One mile at a time. One breath at a time.

*****

After my first panic attack, my perspective morphed again. I started to see work differently, I started to see nursing differently. Yet again. I didn't feel the same way walking into work as I previously did. The trauma was back, and I didn't feel safe anymore. I was anticipating the next bad thing to happen that would send me into survival mode again. My fight-or-flight mode was constantly in overdrive. PTSD activated yet again.

Grief has a way of trapping you. You're swimming to the surface, almost ready to escape that harsh current of the ocean that is pulling you down, but grief is like the anchor at the bottom of the ocean. You're attached to it. It's not going anywhere. You can swim upwards all you want, but that anchor is still there. You're tied to it. And for a while there you're swimming up and you don't even feel the rope. It's not tugging you down. You're swimming upwards peacefully, but

Boom! That rope tied to your ankle stops you dead in your tracks and reminds you, "Hey, I'm still here. I'm not going anywhere!"

*****

Don't ever gamble on the weather but I just
watch while the
The sun is shinin', I can look at the horizon
The walls keep gettin' wider, I just hope I never
find 'em, no, no
Yeah, well
These are my wings
These are my wings
These are my wings
(Mac Miller, "Wings")

Chicago Marathon 2024: mile 8.

I'm still running. Hypervigilance kicks in. I become extremely conscious of my heart rate, my breathing, and my pace. I am going way too fast. I need to slow down. I'm not going to make it to the end of the race if I continue this pace. The excitement has passed. I need to listen to my body now. My rapid breathing indicates that I am running too fast for my breath to keep pace with. Slow it down.

*****

Breathe. Breathe. Breathe.

*****

I spend a lot of time in prayer after this panic attack. I was taking medication for anxiety and PTSD, but as witnessed, this alone is not enough to fix this disorder. I needed to search deeper. I needed to face these triggers head-on and defeat them so that I could function again. I had to change my brain mechanisms. I could not rely on the medications I was on to prevent panic attacks. Yes, they help immensely. But similar to how I couldn't depend on my job at Northwestern, I could not depend on these medications either.

I had no choice, I needed to give up control, again. But not give up control to the trauma. I had to somehow transform this loss of control into something positive, something hopeful, something that would last. I had to give up control to that higher power. The one that was always present. The one that was most prevalent when I met Arash, the one that was most prevalent when I stepped off the plane in Ireland, the one that was most prevalent in telling me to leave Northwestern. The one that was with me on my run on the Prairie Path and my walk by the Lakeshore Path. The one that allowed me to see that positive pathway with Arash on his last few days. That power was always present; I just wasn't always listening to it.

Reflecting on that panic attack, I had tried to control the situation. I ran into Rosemary-Connelly unaware of the situation at hand, and my first reaction was to try and control it. I will step up and be the one to call 911. I will be the one to make this right, I know what the best course of action is right now. Again, I, I, I...

Yes, I needed to react. I was a nurse in an emergency situation. I needed to react for the resident. But my initial reaction was to silence that higher power's voice and take the lead myself. I don't know what the higher power would have told me to do in that situation, because I didn't listen to it. I listened to my own ego. And it created extreme contradiction in my brain, which led to extreme physical discomfort.

I had to change the way I thought. The resident having a seizure at Rosemary-Connelly was out of my control. But my thoughts were telling me to try to control it. My body physically told me that I no longer can keep thinking like this or I was not going to make it.

But how do you change the way you think?

First, I needed to stop making protecting my ego my highest priority. I was letting all situations, all conversations, all circumstances be centered around my ego. I had a large pill to swallow. I had to face it: it's not about me. I needed to push my ego to the back of my brain. I needed to get over myself.

*****

126

"A little hypocritical there, Meg." Arash laughs.
A yellow butterfly tickles his ear.

*****

I think it's unnatural to think this way. At least it is for me.

When I was working at Northwestern and I was facing criticism from my peers, my instinct was to protect my ego at all costs. I was a new addition to their spine team. I was on orientation. Isn't the whole point of orientation for your preceptors and mentors to critique your skills and to give you constructive feedback so you can improve your performance? But at the time, I didn't see it that way. I saw it as a personal attack to my character. What they were telling me was contraindicating with my perception of my fragile ego at the time. Enter fight-or-flight mode: protect ego for survival.

I think grief has a way of revealing our ego. You are told to take the time to grieve so you can take care of yourself. The pull of the anchor at the bottom of the ocean is the heaviest during grief. You have to protect yourself from being pulled all the way to the bottom. And you do this by taking the necessary steps to stay afloat. You need to eat, you need to sleep, you need to cope. Basically you need to survive. There's no time or room for really anything besides that. You need to beat that first heavy initial pull of that anchor. So you do, you swim up, and you survive. I think this is a learned brain mechanism. Repeated behavior sticks. For a solid year, my brain was in grieving mode. Eat, sleep, cope. Repeat. And that was okay. My ego was trying to protect myself from the trauma and pain.

I think it takes time for our brain to unlearn those mechanisms. Just like it took time for your brain to build the mechanisms to protect itself, it takes time for your brain to unlearn these hypervigilant ways of protecting itself from the trauma and grief.

Instead of looking at the criticism as an attack on my character, maybe I need to change the way I think about criticism. I need to realize that criticism is a completely separate concept than my ego. These are two separate things. Yes, they affect each other. But one is not dependent on the other. I think that's what I struggled with. I equated my self-worth with criticism and other's opinions and perspectives of me. In my brain, they were dependent on each other. But in reality, these are two completely different concepts. I need to start seeing these two things differently. The criticism that we receive from others: whether that be in a job, in school, in friendships, in relationships, etc., is a result of circumstantial, personal, and societal factors and influences.

Essentially, it's similar to the ocean. Imagine you are swimming upward in the ocean. You have that rope tied around your ankle, and it is attached to the anchor at the bottom of the ocean. This could be at a time where the anchor's pull is heavy such as when you're going through grief or a rough season in life, such as losing a loved one, a job, etc., or it could be at a time where the anchor's pull is light such as when you're experiencing a good season in life, like a new job, a new opportunity, a new relationship, a new baby, etc. That swim upwards is going to be affected by other fish in the ocean; it's going to be affected by other currents. Sometimes you'll be swimming in alignment with other fishes' currents, sometimes you won't. But you have to keep in mind that all other creatures in the sea have their own anchors to deal with. So their current or criticism can affect your journey. It should and it will. However, you need the currents of other fish in the sea to keep moving. But these currents don't change the fact that the rope (or your fragile ego) is still tied to your ankle. No other fishes' current or criticism, however extreme, can change that.

When your main priority is protecting your ego or the rope tied around your ankle, you are not going to move upwards towards the shore. You can't. Because if you value your fragile ego more than you value adapting, learning, and growing from the changing currents or criticism, feedback, opinions of others, then you will spend your time holding on to that rope around your ankle, trying to protect it at all costs. And after time, you will become exhausted. Your fragile ego is but a drop in the infinity of the ocean. You cannot hold your foot still in the ever-changing ocean. There will always be currents.

So I slowly release my grip from holding on to that rope. It is scary. It took a lot of pain and trauma to get there. But without that pain, you wouldn't even have an anchor in the first place.

Chicago Marathon: mile 11.

I am tired. My motivation is beginning to decrease. I'm not even halfway there yet! Adjust your focus. Focus on the continuous crowd of runners. You can't stop now! There's too many people running forward around you. It would take more energy to weave through these people to get to the side of the race. It would take more energy to exit through that gate and then move through that sea of people. So you keep running.

Arash chuckles. "Yeah, Meg, & you'd look like a running back." The yellow butterfly lands on his nose.

Chapter 9

Going Backwards? Part 2

Phew. So now that I am loosening my grip from that rope tied to my ankle, I can start to swim to the top of the ocean again. My fragile ego is not going to weigh me down anymore. I make a conscious decision to loosen my grip and let go of my insecurities, my defensiveness, my pride, my vanity. This is a learned brain mechanism. It took a year of painful grieving for me to get to this point of grasping so tightly on to this ego, this identity, this crutch, this imaginary safety net. It's going to take time to learn that I need to make a conscious decision every day that this is no longer my priority. I need to wake up every morning and actively decide that I am not holding on to this for dear life anymore. Yes, the trauma still exists. Yes, like the ocean, this grief's pull on me will come in waves, but I am deciding that I am ready to fight back. I am ready to live again. I am ready to swim to the top of the ocean and to learn and grow from the currents that I will face. I am ready.

*****

Now that I have made this decision. It's time to start swimming upwards towards the surface. My next challenge will be learning how to navigate through these currents.

This is not my first time navigating through these currents. I have been doing it my whole life, I just wasn't necessarily aware of it. For a while in life, I was just treading in the water. No real foundation. And when you don't have a real foundation, you are only swayed by the current, or the perspectives, criticisms, opinions of others and of society. This was a learned brain mechanism over years of life, so it's going to take work to unlearn this and truly learn to swim through the currents. So I'm really going to try to be patient with myself.

I need to change the way I think about the currents. I need to train my brain to think differently. This is not easy. You are fighting generations and generations of suffering, pain, violence, abuse, and disease. You are fighting against your subconscious. This is no easy feat. Your brain is about to go to war. But you are strong. You have a foundation in that pathway.

*****

Arash smiles. "You got this." The yellow butterfly is now on the ground, about to start its journey of learning how to fly.

*****

These currents aren't prohibiting. They are not disabling. They are necessary. These are not bad, they are challenges. Good challenges. They can be fun; they can be adventurous. They can force you to go out of your comfort zone, but that's okay. These are good things. They have nothing to do with the rope wrapped around your ankle.

*****

Panic Attack 2

At Misericordia, the residents will typically go home for "home visit" weekends and for holidays. Their family members will pick them up and bring them to their home for these long weekends and holidays. Christmastime is the biggest home visit weekend. Shannon

Apartments is closed for a week while residents go home to be with their families.

The residents return to Shannon Apartments, and I am sitting in the nursing office, charting. I receive a phone call from the Director of Nursing.

She begins to explain to me that she had just received a phone call that one of the residents from Shannon Apartments had a heart attack while he was at home visiting his family in Ohio. He was in the hospital for a few days. Thankfully, he is okay. She says to me, "Megan, this could have been prevented."

Activate PTSD, activate fight or flight. Activate "Protect ego at all costs."

I hang up the phone in utter disbelief. And then it begins: I can feel the panic attack coming. That rope that is tied around my ankle is getting tighter and tighter. That anchor is trying to win. I go into a panic attack; this one so severe I actually had to leave work and go home.

Now that I am looking at other's perspectives, criticisms, comments, opinions, and values of me differently, I will look try to look at this current differently.

In the moment, I was angry again. That defense mechanism kicks in. "How in the world could this have been prevented?!?!"

Instead of reaching down to that rope to protect my ego, first I'll look at it differently. Could this have been prevented? No. I need to have grace with myself. I need to remember the pathway when Arash was days away from his last breath. Remembering that pathway, I come to terms that I am not in control. That spiral of defensiveness and self-loathing in the past just doesn't make sense anymore. It's pointless.

Next, now that I have accepted that this is not my fault. This truly could not have been prevented. I need to extend this same grace that the pathway has given me and give grace to my boss. I need to recognize that she is dealing with her own currents. Maybe she's in a time of a harsh current.

Deep breath, and keep swimming.

*****

Something needed to change. My mental health was completely deteriorating. It was no longer healthy for me to continue working at Misericordia. Again, I will not make it if I continue on like this. But like the currents in the ocean, you keep moving. You have no choice. The infinity of the ocean is stronger than you are.

I arrive home after this panic attack, and Emily is working at her computer.

Emily is a beautiful human being. She is kind and funny, and she's the greatest friend you'll ever have. Emily had seen me at some of my darkest moments in the year after Arash passed. She is a great friend and truly wants what's best for everyone around her. She saw how much I was struggling. She listened to me vent about Northwestern, and now, she was seeing how much of a toll Misericordia had taken on me.

Emily's father works in medical sales and frequents the Rush Operating Room. She advocates for Rush, stating her father has had a great experience there and notices how happy the nurses are there and how positive the environment is. I, too, have heard this from friends and acquaintances that work at Rush.

Her father gave me a contact for the Rush Operating Room, and I interview with them. They extend an opportunity to shadow the Rush Operating Room, and I accept this.

"What's the definition of insanity?"

Was I going to return to the operating room after I had left a year prior for unsettling reasons? Could I even still do this anymore? Could I still even do *any* job anymore? This is now two jobs that I am leaving within two years. My self-worth and self-confidence were at an all-time low. I was grasping that rope around my ankle still.

But what do you do? You keep swimming, you have no choice. The current is still moving.

Maybe Rush will be different, I tell myself. I remind myself of my initial passion for the operating room. I console myself with reminding myself that I was grieving when I was at Northwestern. It was too personal. It was too close to home. It was two months after Arash had passed away.

So I give it a chance.

> See this in 3D
> All lights out for me, All lights out for me.
> Lightning strikes the beach.
> 80 degrees. Warm it up for me
> Finally free, found the God in me
> & I want you to see, I can walk on water
> Thousand miles from shore, I can float on water
> Father, hold me close don't let me drown
> I know you won't
> (The Weekend and Kanye West, "Hurricane," *Donda*)

Flashback 5: Charleston, South Carolina

As I sit on Coronado Beach in San Diego, California, and I look out onto the Pacific Ocean, I see a ship across the sea.

My mind is transported back to when Arash and I went to Charleston, South Carolina, for a weekend trip. Arash scheduled a boat tour on the Atlantic Ocean. We had just gotten breakfast, and now we are running down the pier to make sure we can board the boat in time. We are cutting it close. Only five minutes until the boat sets sail. We make it in the nick of time. As we catch our breaths and take a seat, the boat takes off into the Atlantic Ocean. The wind is breezing through our hair. We are in love. I look to Arash as he smiles and puts his arm around me.

We are surrounded by other tourists on this boat, but they start to fade from our vision. The tour guide is talking over the intercom, but it soon starts to be drowned out by the sound of the waves crashing. All I can see in this moment is Arash's smile. I feel at peace, knowing that I'll be with him for the rest of the weekend. This peace warms my heart.

The boat continues to sail through the Atlantic Ocean, and yellow butterflies emerge from the water and fill the boat.

That weekend is just beginning.

*****

Chicago Marathon 2023: mile 14.

Okay, you are more than halfway through. You are entering the second half of the marathon! You got this. You can do it. The hardest part is over. You completed the first half, now you are starting the final half. I remember in that moment all the long runs I completed on the Lakeshore Path all summer. And one idea specifically sticks out: whenever I would look out onto the Lakeshore Path, there was a ship out in the distance. This ship was always there. No matter what. It reminds me of that bliss Arash and I experienced in South Carolina. That happened, that was real.

Whenever I would reach those final miles in my long runs, I would look to my left and see that ship in the distance. It was always there. Always. It never changed. It didn't matter how exhausted I was. It didn't matter how I felt about that particular run, if I looked to my left, it was there. I could have had the best run and enter those final miles feeling good or I could have been completely drained entering those final miles, if I looked to my left, it was there.

It was there every single time. Without fail. Every time. Maybe this could be my new anchor at the bottom of the ocean?

Chapter 10

Going Backwards? Part 3

I am shadowing Rush's OR today. This is great! I took the morning off work at Misericordia and had plans to shadow the OR from 8:00 a.m. to 12:00 p.m. and then return to work at Misericordia from 1:00 p.m. to 4:00 p.m. Regardless of whether I take this position, it'll be a good experience to keep my options open. It'll be good to see a new workplace. To experience something new. To know that I don't have to stay in this cycle of trauma. There was hope again.

*****

I arrive at Rush's OR and meet with the nursing director; she is pleasant and encouraging. She asked me what my previous specialty was when I worked in the operating room prior. I told her that my specialty was spine/neurosurgery. She asked me if I wanted to shadow in a spine room or if I wanted to shadow in another room.

"Hmm… I'll try something new."

A yellow butterfly appears again.

*****

I am shadowing in a cardiovascular surgery. I feel at ease.

There is just something about the operating room that has always lit a passion in me. The fast pace is exhilarating. The teamwork and long hours lead to a strong sense of community. Everyone in that room has one goal: to do the best for the patient. The stakes are high. The egos are big. You feel confident. Each surgery case is an act. It has the opening act, the main performance, and the closing act. But the closing act is always the same. And that you can rely on.

But can you?

I had now been on the other side of the OR perspective. The patient's side.

Still, the only thing you can rely on is that pathway. I had watched the operating room fail. Maybe not in the actual operating room, but I had witnessed the aftermath of the patient waking up from that anesthesia and returning home just for things to stay the same. Correction, things to actually get worse. The inevitable pathway was coming. No surgery, no doctor, no medicine, and no magic surgery or chemotherapy pill could change that. This pathway that I had seen as traumatic and painful for so long had changed in my mind. Similar to the currents you have to face to get there, the pathway is good.

Chapter 11

California Part 5

There's beauty in that traumatic journey. It's here where you learn what you're made of. You don't gain character, perseverance, or grit when everything in your life is going perfectly. You are never closer to God than when you are suffering. & through him you can do all things.

"With man this is impossible, but with God all things are possible" (Matthew 19:26).

I am sitting with my toes in the sand at Pacific Beach. The sun is lighting up my face. My skin is burning a little, but it's okay. My body needed this. It reminds me of the pain that used to be my main focus. Now I am making an active choice to not focus on my burning skin but to look to my left. On my left is the Pacific Beach boardwalk. There are multiple little huts on this boardwalk. They sit on top of wooden pillars that are holding up the huts and the pathway. This pathway goes forward, it stretches into the ocean. These wooden pillars are steady. They are dependable. They stand perfectly steady as the ocean waves continue to splash against them. This foundation is not going anywhere. That pathway is not going anywhere. No matter what the currents may bring.

Chapter 12

Breaking Point Part 1

I leave Rush's OR and make my drive back to Misericordia. I had an appointment with my psychiatrist at noon. I typically take these phone calls in the basement lounge of Shannon Apartments.

As I'm walking into Shannon Apartments, I pick up the phone call from my psychiatrist as I am making my way down the hall past my office to the staircase leading to the basement. While I am on this call, I look into my office. The lights were completely off, but I could see the outlines of people in my office. The outlines looked like the tracings of people. One person was sitting at my desk, and one was sitting at the chair next to my desk. They were sitting in complete darkness.

I see this in the corner of my vision as I am hustling to the basement on the phone with my psychiatrist.

Fight-or-flight mode activated. I push these images to the back of my mind, I am on the phone with my psychiatrist. I am safe. I continue to the basement lounge, open the door, and take a seat at a chair. I am the only one in the lounge.

My psychiatrist asked me how I've been doing. I told her about the previous panic attack. I tell her about the resident who was on home visit in Ohio who suffered from a heart attack about a week prior. I told her the whole story and how this panic attack was so severe I had to leave work. I explained the fear that this was causing me.

After this conversation, I walked upstairs to my office, and the resident who had suffered from the heart attack in Ohio was sitting in my office. He had complaints of a headache and was sent home from his work on the other side of campus to see the nurse.

PTSD overload. The paranoia overwhelms my body. The trauma floods my brain. The screaming at Arash's funeral, the sounds of the sirens overwhelm my ears. I can only see Arash's face lying in a casket. I can only see the morbid makeup on his face. These images engulf my vision. I can smell his musty, dry breath on his last day of life. My breath becomes shallow, I need to leave. I need to exit. Immediately. I am not safe. I need air. It takes all my strength to continue to breathe. Death is all I can see.

Breaking point. I'm done. I leave Misericordia. That was my last day.

*****

I've never cried when I was feeling down
I've always been scared of the sound
Jesus don't love me, no one ever carried my load
I'm too young to feel this old
(Kings of Leon, "Cold Desert")

*****

Arash lies next to me on the beach while I write this. He is on a long blue beach towel. His shirt is off. He is wearing a pair of red swimming trunks. His hairy chest is facing the sky. He just moved his sunglasses off his face and is taking in the eternity of the sun. He is embracing it. His body is so illuminated.

"Oh, come on, Meg, it wasn't that bad." Arash chuckles.

Many yellow butterflies land all over his sun-kissed skin. His skin is glittering in the sun.

Part 3

Healing

Chapter 1

Changing

My coworkers had seen this panic attack, and some had seen the one prior. People were concerned for me. I received many calls and texts after I left Misericordia that day to check in and see how I was doing. Many people sent me prayers and best wishes. I had a conversation with my manager about what happened, and I was gut-level honest in telling her that I had mental health issues that were becoming disabling. I was not sure if I could return to work, and I needed to take some time. She is very kind and supportive of this and tells me to reach out to Human Resources for FMLA paperwork.

FMLA paperwork? FMLA as in the FMLA that I took a year prior to when Arash passed away? No. No. This can't be happening. I'm not sick. They're the problem. Not me. My heart rate increases while I write this. I wasn't ready to give up. I wasn't ready to take that last breath at the top of the ocean. There's more growth for me in the beautiful and painful currents of this life.

I sat with this for a while. I'm finding now it's best to let things simmer. What's the rush? The worry, the anxiety, the fear. It's present. It'll always be present. I'm well aware of that. It's the anchor at the bottom of the ocean that is slowly changing to a ship each and every day. So why rush it? Why not take the time to really, truly think about this? Why do we force ourselves to live so aggressively?

Work calls again and again, pressing me to see if and when I could return. But I make a conscious choice. I chose to take the time to listen to the higher power, to find that pathway again and sit with Him and speak with Him. I chose to listen this time.

I haven't had a panic attack since.

Okay, let me try to change my brain mechanisms again to process this situation in terms of the positive pathway. Not the traumatic one.

First, I focus on this positive path. I remember that even when pure evil is right next to you, the pathway is still sitting right over there. It's ahead of you. I picture Arash's hand reaching out to me. I picture the best friend I've ever had sitting at the trunk of a tree. I remember the complete and perfect love that was demonstrated and received in those final days. That happened. That was real. That's the truth. Next, I remember that Arash is safe. Next, I need to recognize that Arash saw this pathway first. But he himself is not the pathway. But he saw it first. So I can cling on to these memories to warm me when I'm cold, to cheer me up when I'm down, to motivate me, and to inspire me. But I cannot idolize these memories above all else. I need to idolize the pathway. First and foremost. Always. Arash would want me to. He was baptized.

Second, I remember that the trauma of this event is the anchor at the bottom of the ocean, but as Arash saw first, there is the ship that is out in the ocean. There is hope and there is life despite the horrible circumstances going on around you. And each and every day, that anchor is slowly changing to a ship. But now that we know the truth of the perfect love that was both demonstrated and received, we know that ships sail on water. So we can now morph our perspective to see us swimming toward that ship. It is now our main motivator. It's not the anchor/trauma at the bottom of the ocean anymore. We're not swimming away from the anchor anymore, we're swimming up toward the ship. Let's focus on that from now on. He did the work which allowed us to. We can look at the ship now. We do not have to feel guilty, ashamed, or alone anymore. He would not want us to. Let's look at the ship.

Third, now that we have been blessed to look at the world differently, we can make conscious decisions that help us swim upward toward the ship. Our choices are no longer going to be made to prevent the anchor from pulling us down. Because that anchor is now a ship up above us. But we still have that rope tied around our ankles. Our egos are not going anywhere. But as this anchor loses its weight to move upward in the ocean and transform into the ship, that rope will follow. It will be slower than the transformation of the anchor. It'll wade behind the anchor as it moves upward. So now we can stop making decisions to protect our ego and instead make decisions to transform our ego to battle the ever-changing, ever-challenging currents on the way up to becoming a ship.

*****

I sat with this decision for a long time, and I tried to listen, but I didn't hear much. I did the things that I had done in the past when I was REALLY trying to listen. I ran, I prayed, I drove. I spent time with family and friends. But still nothing really comes to mind. No inspiration. No direction. Nothing.

I think this is the hardest part. The waiting. I waited so long while Arash was sick to finally hear something. But when I did finally hear Him and I finally saw the pathway, everything made sense.

A yellow butterfly stands perfectly still.

*****

So naturally, another challenge occurs in the waiting period: my drinking. I cannot believe it took me until part 3 of this book to even mention it. Maybe that's how much I was in denial. Maybe that's how many generations drinking had been passed down in my family, in my genetics, in my heritage. After Arash passed, this was absolutely the biggest challenge. The challenge of changing my relationship with drinking and diverging from the rocky road of substance abuse that I was headed down was harder than any of the challenges I faced at Elmhurst, Northwestern, or Misericordia.

I'm 90% Irish. Maybe 10% Scottish.

Drinking has been such a part of my family and heritage for as long as I remember, I never thought about it. I just did it. We're Irish, it's what we do. Reflecting on this, when I wrote about trauma at the beginning of the book and I listed war, violence, abuse, etc., etc., I am realizing that drinking was my trauma. That existed even before I met Arash. It was my way and my family's way of coping with anxiety, restlessness, agitation, and depression that had been passed down from generations of war and violence in Ireland. Again, I think this is universal. Every culture has their own version of coping with that same anxiety, restlessness, agitation, war, violence, and depression—that trauma that's been passed on throughout generations. It's in every culture. It's that internal war that has existed inside of us for even longer than we've been alive.

So when those feelings of loneliness or numbness were too painful, I drank. A lot. It took my love breaking up with me to realize that. It took my brother getting arrested while out drinking with me to finally realize that I could no longer continue on like this. If I keep abusing alcohol, I will not make it.

As I have learned from the past two years, I myself do not have the power to change this on my own. So I needed to look at Him for the pathway. I needed to change the way I thought about drinking. But as we know, like all patterns, this was a learned brain mechanism over time, so now, I need to unlearn that brain mechanism.

First, I focus on the pathway.

Second, I need to focus on the peaceful pathway, NOT the traumatic pathway. My family had been drinking a lot, and we had just gone through something traumatic, so naturally we relied on our coping mechanisms to get through the hard time. That is okay. When you're going through grief or trauma, your lows are going to be lower and your highs are going to be higher. I needed to accept this and recognize that He forgave me so I can now forgive myself. I will not go down a spiral of self-loathing. That's pointless and a waste of time. There is no point of beating yourself up for leaning on your coping mechanisms in a time of grief. It's human nature. You did that to survive.

Third, now that I realize that drinking is a trauma that was the anchor at the bottom of the ocean, I can see drinking in a different light now. The anchor that I once saw as permanently attached to the bottom of the ocean has been freed. It took intense trauma and intense pain, but it is freed. That is the truth. It took pain and suffering, but that traumatic pathway was changed to a peaceful pathway. So now when I think about drinking, I will see it as that anchor or that trauma. It's not a coping mechanism for survival anymore, it is the trauma itself. But now that we have established that the truth is that this anchor was meant to turn to a ship all along, we can slowly let this trauma lose its heaviness and float to the top of the ocean. It's not our foundation anymore.

Chapter 2

Changes

Day 2 of the drive. Destination: Richfield, Utah.

The fog finally dissipated after leaving Denver. The sun was now coming out from behind the clouds and begins to shine. It illuminates the highway in front of you. It's just you and the road at this point. I had just dropped my mother off at the airport, and I am entering unchartered territory at this point. I have never driven this far west before.

Turn the radio up. You're about to drive to California!

*****

Arash smiles. "You got this, Meg." A yellow butterfly lands in the passenger seat.

*****

The drive through Colorado to Utah is absolutely stunning. I have never seen anything like this before. You are driving on a winding road through mountains so tall and so beautiful words really can't do it justice. To your left are tall rocky mountains that are lightly dusted with snow. To your right are the Rocky Mountains that are lightly dusted with snow. Balance. You are driving on a winding road that is swerving perfectly through these mountains. There is only one lane of traffic moving forward and only one lane of traffic moving past you.

You are in the current of the ocean, you have found the balance. You are finally moving in sync with the current of the ocean.

*****

So if you're tired of the same old story
Oh, turn some pages
I'll be here when you are ready
To roll with the changes
Yeah, yeah, whoo
(REO Speedwagon, "Roll with the Changes")

*****

I am on a complete high. I have never felt so good before. The world is beautiful, God is good. Look at these mountains! How could there not be a good infinity waiting for you at the end of this? The evidence is everywhere. It is in this moment that I realize this beauty couldn't have been possible without the trauma and pain it took to get here. The beauty of this drive is so divine it is in that moment I am completely conscious of God's presence.

It's simple. There's no way this level of beauty could exist without His higher power. Trauma can't compare. Humankind can't compare.

*****

"I'm home now.
Don't be too anxious baby, I swear
Just, the terminal is 5. It'll say the gates when you
get there
And you take one of the escalators up to
Gate 5–6 is right there. And you'll go through
security
Love you, baby"
(An ambulance / fire truck siren goes off in the
background)
"Anyways, I'm rambling now.
Hear the sound of the fire trucks?
That's how you know, I'm officially back home
Can't wait to have you back home. Love you. Bye."
(Voicemail from Arash on June 27, 2021)

*****

Hour 6. I am leaving Colorado and entering Utah. Only a few more hours until Richfield. This is the halfway point from Denver to San Diego.

While I'm driving, I notice my gas is about three-fourths a tank. I remember my dad's advice: "Never let the tank get below halfway."

I continue driving. I pass a gas station. I am fine, I have plenty of gas. I'm good to go. I think to myself.

I drive on.

I pass another gas station. I am fine! I have a little above half a tank, I'm okay. I'm good to go still.

I drive on.

I pass another gas station shortly after. I'm at half a tank; I'm fine. I'm on a roll. I'm lost in the music. I'm good to go.

I drive on.

I pass another gas station. I'm slightly lower than half a tank at this point. I'm fine! Except this time, I hear my father's voice: "Don't let the tank get below halfway." This persists. *I should stop*, I think.

Similar to the incident speeding with the undercover cop earlier, I begin to have another internal conflict. "Should I stop at this next gas station?"

My ego wins this battle. I made a conscious decision to not listen to that higher power. I decided that I was feeling so good and so confident I am going to trust my ego and continue to drive. I have enough gas. I don't need to stop for a little while.

*****

I continue to drive.

I keep driving. The tank is getting lower and lower...

Okay, the next gas station, I will definitely stop at, I think to myself.

I keep driving.

And driving.

I don't see any gas stations in sight. I begin to start worrying. I am in the middle of nowhere. If I run out of gas, I will be stranded on the side of the road. I don't think my phone could even make a phone call out here.

I am reminded of that trauma. I feel its strength slightly pulling me down. My ego won that battle. And because my ego had won, the rope grasps my ankle slightly tighter, trying to pull me down to that anchor.

I keep driving. I have no choice. I have to keep swimming. Because I had lost the battle to my ego, I now will have to weather this current with more difficulty because that rope is grasping my ankle tighter than usual. The anchor is stronger than the ship.

I keep driving, and I pass a sign that says "No services for 40 miles."

Yikes. I look at my gas tank, and I see a little more than a quarter tank. I pull out my phone and try to GPS the closest gas station to me.

Reflecting, what is the point of that? How is me trying to find the closest gas station going to fix the actual problem I'm experiencing?

Is the problem that I'm concerned I'm going to run out of gas? No. I knew that my car's tank had at least 40 miles left in it. The empty light hadn't even turned on.

Okay, so I know this. Why am I still experiencing discomfort? Why am I still nervous, frightened, anxious, and on edge now?

The problem was that I had a conflict with that higher power. He had told me that I should stop at that gas station, and I made a conscious decision to choose my ego over Him.

So I drive.

That anxiety and fear increase and starts to pull me down towards the anchor.

*****

Chicago Marathon: mile 16.

This is the hardest mile of the marathon. I'm not sure why. I'll never know why. But that's okay. Trust what you know. Trust the truth. Trust the training. Trust the plan. Trust His plan. Keep running.

*****

This time, it's different. Yes, I made a mistake. I chose my ego over listening to Him.

But let's use the new brain mechanisms to analyze this.

First, look at the positive pathway.

Second, I recognize I made a mistake. Let's not waste any time. We know the truth. He has forgiven us for these mistakes after generations of trauma. It is pointless to waste time. We're way past that. That is amateur behavior.

Third, I make a conscious decision to focus on the infinity of this road I am driving on. I am kicking that trauma to the bottom of the ocean, and I feel good about it. And I should!

*****

An ambulance passes me on the highway and merges in front of me on the highway. I follow this ambulance as I drive the next 40 miles. There are no sirens going off, there are no lights shining. It is cruising at the same speed as the other cars on the highway.

What once would have caused trauma and PTSD no longer does. I now look at this ambulance as being safe. I find peace in following this ambulance.

*****

Arash smiles at me from the back of the ambulance and waves to me. "Don't worry, baby. We're here if you need it." The yellow butterflies fill my car as I approach the gas station.

*****

I arrive in Utah safely. I am conscious that parts of Utah are "dry" towns—where alcohol sales are illegal.

Chapter 3

Interview, Part 1

Today I have a job interview for an operating room nurse job in San Diego.

What's the definition of insanity? Doing the same thing over and over and expecting a different outcome?

This time. It is different. I woke up today and made a conscious decision that I am choosing the ship over the trauma. My relationship with trauma and that anchor has changed. It has morphed to that hopeful ship out on the horizon that Arash saw first. I am reflecting on both of my experiences in the operating room: the positive one at Elmhurst Hospital and the negative one at Northwestern Hospital.

In preparation for this interview, I am consciously deciding to look at my brain mechanisms prior to going to this interview.

First, I look at the positive pathway. It's sitting right over there. He's not going anywhere.

Second, I recognize that my relationship with trauma and that anchor has changed. It has morphed into that hopeful ship out on the horizon that Arash saw first. When I had the negative experience at Northwestern's Operating Room, I am recognizing that was at a season in my life when I was still attached to that anchor at the bottom of the ocean. The rope around my ankle was extremely tight. I remember the journey that it took for the traumatic pathway to be turned to a peaceful pathway by Him, so I forgive myself quickly. You don't have the time to waste! Of course, when I reflect on this time, the criticism and doubt of my peers at Northwestern resurfaces. I can feel the rope trying to tug on my ankle, but I am making a conscious decision not to grab on to it. He did the work so that pathway could be sitting across the room from me. There is no point of spiraling into self-loathing behavior. Again, we are waaaaaaay past that. We are strong because of this pathway. This pathway cannot be taken away from us no matter what happens at this interview. And we should feel good about this!

Next, now that we have decided not to grab onto that rope at the bottom of our ankle, we are going to start swimming upward in the currents. I recognize that this is an interview. The point of an interview is to be asked questions for interviewers to learn my strengths and weaknesses and to determine if I would be a good fit for the team. It's also an opportunity for me to ask questions and to see if this would be a good fit for me. Knowing this truth, I anticipate that there will be moments of discomfort at this interview. I'm in a current. This current will be affected by the interviewer's ideas, values, and perceptions of me. However, this is just a current. I'll be swimming past it soon. I am consciously deciding that I will use this opportunity to grow. I can learn something from each and every one of the interviewers. I am consciously deciding to enjoy this interview experience regardless of the outcome because I now know the truth that the rope around my ankle will still be present after this interview. The pathway will still be present after this interview. Their questions, their opinions, their judgment in this interview is a completely different concept than the rope tied to my ankle. The rope on my ankle is not dependent on the current anymore. It's dependent on the ship. On the pathway. On our best friend sitting at the trunk of a tree.

Third, when moments of discomfort occur in the interview, first, I will focus on the pathway. Second, I will give them the grace that I first received when I saw the pathway, and third, I will answer the questions to the best of my ability truthfully and honestly so that I can later on make a decision to either continue in this current or recognize there is no growth for me in this current and swim to the next one.

*****

There must be lights burning brighter somewhere
Got to be birds flying higher in a sky more blue
If I can dream of a better land
Where all my brothers walk hand in hand
Tell me why, oh why, oh why can't my dream come true
Oh why
(Elvis Presley, "If I Can Dream")

Chapter 4

California, Part 6

They that go down to the sea in ships
That do business in great water,
They see the works of the Lord
And his wonders in the deep

—Psalm 107:23–31

After my operating room interview, I drove to Coronado Beach. When I parked my car to walk over, this above Bible verse was painted on the front door of the house next to me.

I love driving in California. I feel as if the cars are all in sync. They speed up and they slow down so gracefully. Kind of like birds flying through the sky. You kind of lose yourself while you're driving here. Any mistakes or mishaps seem to fade and disappear when you get on the road. When you look on either side of you and see the California hills, you're reminded of eternity, and that mistake you just made slowly starts to fade away into the infinity of it all.

Maybe it's all really not that bad.

Chapter 5

Interview, Part 2

I completely bomb the first question of the interview. I quite literally answer the exact opposite of what the right answer is. My interviewer steps in and corrects me.

I did it again. My ego won the battle. I silenced that higher power's voice immediately and jump into answering the question on my own. I got this. I know the answer. I don't need you for this interview.

But this time, my reaction was different. I didn't get defensive when the interviewer corrected me. I immediately kick down that rope that's trying to grasp my ankle.

Reflecting on this, my brain is finally starting to make these new mechanisms a pattern. I am aware of the journey and the time it took to get here. It did not happen overnight, and it is a working progress each and every day. In each and every situation. In every current.

Instead of getting defensive and immediately grasping for that rope, I made a conscious decision to focus on the pathway. Again, it's sitting right across the room from me. It's my best friend sitting at the tree trunk. So immediately I focus on this. I immediately give grace to myself and the interviewer.

You're in an interview, you don't have time for that anchor! It's pointless!

So I focus on the ship, and I keep swimming. You're in a current, you don't have a choice!

I actually felt physically different after making this choice in the interview. After I made this choice, I felt a sense of calmness come over me. Now I can relax. Now I can breathe. That initial heavy tug of the anchor has passed. Now I can be myself and enjoy this interview.

I go on to answer the next questions to the absolute best of my ability. I enjoy speaking with both interviewers, and I learn about their favorite part of their jobs and the surgery center.

At the end of the interview, I shake their hands and make my way out of the building.

This current has passed.

While I'm driving home after this, I begin to analyze the interview, both the good parts and the bad parts. I focus on the pathway, and this time, it's easier. I chose to focus on the ship almost immediately.

I don't know if they will call me back for an offer. But that's okay. My ankle is still tied to the ship.

On my drive home, I look out the window and see a yellow butterfly fluttering.

*****

Arash smiles. "You're on the right track, Meg. It might take some time though. Be patient."

Chapter 6

Divine Love

I am now realizing the magnitude of the journey that Arash had gone on before I even met him: when he experienced his first brain tumor. He was unlike anyone I had ever met before because he saw this pathway before anyone else I knew had. This journey is what made him Arash. A loving, kind, compassionate human being. Sometimes in our relationship, I would get frustrated with him because we were ALWAYS moving. We were always doing something, always exploring, always planning the next trip. We never sat still. Maybe this was because Arash had seen the peaceful pathway and he was so eager and willing to follow it.

Chapter 7

Breaking Point, Part 2

I had left Misericordia, and I was listening for guidance for where to go from here. I was waiting for the next step to take in life. I was slowly releasing my grasp on that rope, and I was slowly making my way up the current. The influence that the current heavy wave I was in at Misericordia was finally slowing down a bit. I feel like the waiting period is kind of like a test. I think when you reach this point, you face the test of how serious you really are about actually listening and actually following. Are you sincerely ready to give up and REALLY let go on the grasp around your ankle? Do you truly trust Him?

At this point, I was in pain. As I mentioned before, I told my boss about my debilitating mental health issues, and now I was taking the time to just sit and listen.

But what happens when you're just sitting and waiting and trying to listen? You get bored. I was trying my best to listen. I was praying, I was running, I was driving. Nothing. No signs. No direction. No guidance.

So I drank. I used to drink to have fun and socialize with family and friends. But this drinking was different. While Arash was sick, I drank. But even that was different.

This drinking that I was now doing was strictly to cope. There was no pleasure in this anymore. This wasn't the drinking I had done in college to have fun and celebrate. This wasn't the drinking I had done when Arash was sick. It was similar. But when Arash was sick, I had a reason NOT to drink. I had to be there for him. I had to wake up and go to his house every day. I had to be functioning because people were depending on me to show up and be there.

But now, I was drinking in a completely different way. I had NO reason to stop drinking. I was suffering physically, mentally, and spiritually from the trauma. I had no job anymore. I had no real responsibilities anymore. I had no purpose. When the trauma resurfaced, I would have a drink. It would start out as a glass of wine or a cocktail, but I couldn't stop. I drank to black out and completely forget about the trauma. Like I mentioned previously, one night was rock bottom for me. I drank to oblivion. I had never drunk that much or been that drunk in my entire life. I was drinking to see the casket. I was drinking to see the blackness. I was drinking to see death. I was drinking into that traumatic pathway. I got into such a severe fight with the person I loved, and he broke up with me. My brother got arrested that night for being so drunk and getting into a physical altercation with an Uber driver.

The red flashing lights fill my drunken eyes as the cops handcuffed my brother and threw him into the back of a police car. The sirens were piercing my drunken ears. I took that last breath at the top of the ocean. I was in the casket. I was blackness. I was the trauma.

*****

Reflecting on this as I sit in California. My brother was living at home during the year Arash was sick. He was present for most of Arash's decline. He helped with his care when Arash would come over to our house multiple times a week. He visited Arash while he was on hospice, along with my brother Brendan and Shannon. He developed a genuine close friendship with Arash. He was extremely close to this trauma too. He was present when we went on the trip to The Abbey in Lake Geneva. He was there. And to see him get thrown into a cop car like that, to see him be taken to the hospital and to jail for the anger that was pouring out of him, it was heartbreaking. But it was eye-opening.

For the sake of people that I loved, this cannot go on.

I think one of the hardest parts of substance abuse is getting to the point of realization that you're not just hurting yourself, you're hurting others. I think it's easy to accept that as a concept. For example, I know I drank a lot last night and said mean things to my boyfriend. So now he's mad at me. But still, it's about me. Your subconscious is still feeding your ego and saying that you're only affecting yourself. You're lonely. You're depressed. You're anxious. So that somehow makes you feel better because you don't actually understand that you are affecting other people.

The real challenge is facing your ego and saying "I am drinking too much, and it's negatively affecting other people around me. And because it's affecting other people around me, I don't want to abuse alcohol anymore because I value the other people in my life more than I value my own ego."

I think it's easy to continue doing the addictive behavior because your subconscious is telling you that you're only affecting yourself. I am choosing to drink, and I'm dealing with the consequences of my own actions. I am continuing to make bad decisions because I am not happy. I am in pain, I am lonely. I am depressed. I am anxious. Again, I...I...I...

As I mentioned earlier, changing my relationship with drinking was the biggest challenge I had to face after Arash passed away. I'm even struggling now to change my brain mechanisms to find a way to look at drinking a different way so that I won't return to that traumatic pathway. It won't happen overnight. It's a daily battle.

First, I'll look at the pathway. It's sitting right over there, I remind myself. I have to remember this. I have to remind myself of this. Constantly. Because you're in the ocean. It's crazy out there! How do I continue to remind myself of this? I do the activities that I see this pathway the clearest or hear this pathway's voice the loudest. For me, I pray, I run, I drive. The more I do these activities, the more opportunities I give myself to remind me that the pathway is always there. It is a peaceful one. You're always safe. And when you forget about the pathway, the repetition that you build in these activities will train your subconscious to remind you of the pathway when your fragile ego forgets about it.

I think what I struggled with the most with changing my relationship with drinking was that I truly thought the pathway wasn't there when I was drinking. If I was making mistakes, making bad decisions, I truly thought the pathway was either traumatic or simply not present. And as a result, I would grab that rope and be yanked to the bottom because I hadn't seen the ship yet.

Second, I remember that the pathway first appeared to me when evil and trauma were sitting on my left. Arash was sitting next to me gasping for air. That was my anchor. But this anchor was about to transform to a ship. That traumatic pathway that I used to see was now transformed to a peaceful pathway. Arash could not talk. He couldn't walk. He couldn't speak. But he held on to that rosary in his hand for dear life in his last few weeks of life. Arash saw this pathway first. That is real. That happened. That is the truth.

*****

I didn't drink for at least 40 days after that night. Not a sip. Cold turkey. And I can honestly say I didn't want to. That desire was gone. I didn't even crave it. This horrible night occurred on December 21, and I went through the Christmas and New Year's holiday season not drinking a sip. Neither did my parents or my brother. The coping mechanism that I had been using for so long, the coping mechanism that my family had been using for so long, the coping mechanism that had been passed down from my heritage in Ireland after generations and generations of coping with violence, war, disease, and trauma had engulfed me and morphed me into the actual trauma and the actual anchor at the bottom of the ocean so immensely and so entirely that I was finally free.

*****

Arash never really got drunk. He would only have a drink or two and would be completely coherent. Now, I understand why.

*****

Flashback 6:
Detroit, Michigan

Arash and I are at a Detroit Tigers versus Chicago Cubs game with our friends Van and Keekz, and we are sipping on ice-cold beers in the summer sun. We are smiling and laughing and enjoying the game. The Cubs just hit a home run, and we cheers to that!

*****

Drinking doesn't have to be a bad thing.

Flashback 7:
Los Angeles, California

Arash and I are at the Dodgers game in Los Angeles, California. Our seats are in the 200 level directly behind home plate. The Cubs just pitched a perfect game. We clink our ice-cold beers to cheer to a wonderful game! To see a perfect game is a once-in-a-lifetime event!

*****

Drinking can be done in celebration of good things.

*****

Okay, so now I'm going to continue changing my brain mechanisms so that I can see drinking in a different way.

First, I look at the pathway.

Second, I remember that drinking is an anchor at the bottom of the ocean. But it has been changed to a ship. So yes, it's going to take time for that trauma to completely morph into a ship. That trauma also will have to pass through the currents to become a ship. These currents will be challenging at times and enjoyable at times. These currents will be influenced by the other fish. Sometimes, you'll align with the fishes' currents, and other times you won't. Doesn't change the fact that your ego, the rope, is still attached…

Wait.

I just came to the realization that not being able to defeat my ego of I, I, I thinking (or getting out of my head) was the hardest part of changing the way I thought about drinking. I drank because it only affected me. It was my rope. Yes, it wasn't dependent on the currents. But it was affected by the currents. So maybe now I have to face that my ego affects the currents of other fishes. My drinking affects not only me but also the other people around me. And now that I have seen the peaceful pathway and been blessed with this gift, I have a responsibility to care for other fish in the sea as well. After all, we're all in the same crazy ocean trying our best to swim to the top.

This freedom and responsibility excites me! Time to change the world!

*****

Chicago Marathon: mile 19.

I am running. I am running next to my sister and best friend, Shannon. I am exhausted. I am tired. I am struggling. But I start to focus on Shannon. I have to run for her, I have to run with her. If I stop running, she'll stop. If she stops running, I'll stop. We have to do this together. There is just no way we are going to finish these last seven miles without each other. Keep pace with Shannon. Keep breathing.

*****

Yellow butterflies surround us.

*****

Arash is a spectator in the crowd laughing at us. He takes a sip of his beer. "Whose idea was this? I mean, I knew you two were crazy, but…"

Chapter 8

Shannon

I hope that I can do this chapter justice.

Shannon is my twenty-four-year-old sister. She is about five feet five. She is stunning. Literally, she could be a model. She is thin and fit. She has long legs and beautiful thick sandy brown hair. She has fierce bluish-green eyes and the longest eyelashes you will ever see. She is naturally pretty. She truly doesn't need makeup.

Shannon is confident. I've aways admired this about her. She's decisive and assertive. She stands up for herself and what she believes in. She's also the most loyal person you will ever meet. She would go to the trenches for the people she loves. And she has. She graduated from the University of Illinois and made the dean's list. She is studious, hardworking, and successful. She is going places.

Shannon loved Arash. As you can picture, a Caucasian Irish girl dating an Iranian guy is a little far from the norm. Shannon welcomed Arash in immediately. The two shared many common interests and could talk about the classes, parties, and events at U of I. Arash and I even visited Shannon one weekend to go to a U of I basketball game with her. This happened the week before the COVID-19 pandemic hit.

I don't think I leaned on anyone the way I leaned on Shannon during this time. She was there for me through thick and thin. She is strong and supportive. She will tell you what you need to hear even when you don't want to hear it. She wants what's best for you. She has multiple friends and is extremely popular. She's fun. People want to be around her. She's the best sister anyone could ever have. She's my best friend.

She would come visit Arash at his house when he was on hospice care.

Shannon is strong. She is very similar to my mom. I have rarely seen either one of them show extreme emotion. Let alone cry.

*****

Arash and I were living in an apartment on Division Street in Chicago, Illinois. After Arash passed away, we had to go the apartment to clean it out.

My heart is heavy writing this. Cleaning out the apartment of the place you called home with the person you loved...I really, I can't. Forgive me for this one. My eyes are filling up with tears just writing this. Teardrops flood the keys of my laptop.

But like the holy water that was poured over Arash's head during his baptism, these tears can now be washed down into the streets of California and be cleansed in the ocean.

Quick! Remember the pathway. It's right over there. He's right there.

That could have been one of the hardest things I've ever had to do. I can remember this like it was yesterday. My mother, my sister, Shannon, and my brother Sean and I drove in my mom's black Buick from our home in Elmhurst, Illinois, to Chicago, Illinois. We cleaned out the apartment. We went through the closets and packed up clothes.

The couch where we used to sit, the bed we used to sleep on, the shower we used to share, the kitchen counter we used to eat at...

*****

This is the first time in my life I have ever seen Shannon break down crying. It was unsettling and heartbreaking but moving.

*****

Hey, it's trauma here. I'm gonna tighten that rope around your ankle.

Nope. Not happening. Not even a chance. I kick it easily down toward the bottom of the ocean.

Remember His pathway.

*****

Reflecting on this, it was beautiful that Arash allowed my family and me to be part of his journey. He could have easily heard this diagnosis and broken up with me. He could have pushed me away. He could have declined the invitations to our house for holidays. He could have given up on our relationship and given up on our love. But he didn't. He allowed my family to be a part of that. That's truly beautiful.

*****

The only reason I got through that day was because my mom, brother, and sister were there. Now, it is my turn to return the favor.

Chicago Marathon 2024: mile 20.
Shannon turns to me. "Meg, let's run this f——cking thing!"

Chapter 9

Boredom

After I fell in love with Arash and after Arash passed, after leaving two jobs dramatically, after the downward spiral of severe substance abuse, I am listening. I'm a listener now. I am willing and eager to follow that path. I willingly want to follow that path. I want to become a ship. I want to morph my ego into living for other people. Not myself anymore. I am overwhelmed with the love that was shown to me during this dark journey, and I want to repay it.

I am listening.

*****

But I don't hear anything. Yet.

*****

Every now and then, I still get the urge to call up my old friend loneliness for the night. But no. I choose to call freedom tonight.

*****

Okay, so I'm listening but not hearing anything.
Pray. Run. Drive. Listen. Repeat.
Nothing.

I think, *I need to change this thought...*

No, actually, maybe I don't. Maybe I don't need to try and control my thoughts. Maybe I don't need to do anything in this waiting period. Just listen. Truly listen to that higher power that we KNOW exists.

Maybe I just need to vibe with that higher power for a bit. Maybe I need to lighten up a bit. Whatever you're facing, it's going to be okay. So try to enjoy the ups and downs and enjoy the ride.

*****

Arash smiles. "Meg! That's what I've been trying to tell you all along!"

*****

Boredom. It's a tricky thing. It's not a trauma. So what is it?

Boredom. I just googled the definition of *boredom*, and the first thing that comes up is "The state of feeling bored."

What in the??? What does that mean??

I guess boredom is sort of like limbo. You're just sort of wading in the sea. Not in a current. Not really influenced by the anchor or the ship.

When I look at my substance abuse with alcohol, I'm realizing that it was essentially a war against boredom. When I was completely sober, I was in the middle of the ocean wading in the water. Now that I know that drinking is a trauma, and we've already determined that traumas have been defeated through this powerful, positive pathway and are morphing to ships, there is no point in grabbing on to that rope and spiraling down the pathway of self-loathing. We know the pathway is not traumatic. The positive pathway is set in stone. We know this. We're wayyyyy past that. Life is too good. Life is too beautiful. We don't have time to waste it anymore! I can now look at drinking in a different way. I'm going to make a conscious decision that now I'm going to view drinking as a war against boredom.

But what is boredom? How can we fight something that we don't even know what it is? The feeling of being bored? I'm going to make a conscious decision that I'm going to think of boredom as the wading period in the ocean. It's the part of the ocean that is between the currents. It's kind of like when you're not facing any challenges but you're not really growing either. Kind of like just existing when you're numb. But I'm not numb anymore. So now I'm going to think of wading as dancing.

When you're dancing, you're essentially following the rhythm of the music. You're moving your body to that rhythm of the song. So now when I'm wading in the ocean—not in a current, and not really influenced by either the anchor or the ship—I'm going to think of boredom as wading or dancing in the ocean.

And as everyone knows, dancing is the best! That's universal too.

So now when I think of abusing alcohol, of course, I remember the pathway first. Repetition is everything.

Then I recognize that abusing alcohol is a war against boredom.

I'm going to choose to dance. I guess this could really be literally or metaphorically.

Now, I'm in a waiting period, I'm wading in the ocean. I'm listening to that higher power. But haven't heard what my next move is yet. But I'm still in limbo, so I'm wading. I'm dancing to that beautiful song that's playing on that ship at the top of the shore.

Of course, if I face temptation to drink, I can now make a decision that I will have a drink while I'm dancing. I can't get too drunk though because that would mess up my dancing. And it would mess up the dancing of the people next to me. I'm not trying to kill the vibe of this good dance we have going on toward the top. We're dancing, we're vibing, we're listening. There's no rush. He'll speak to us when he's ready and when we're ready. Just enjoy the dancing. You're on the way to the top to hear that final song clearly. That's a guarantee from the pathway.

*****

California Dream 1: I have a dream where I'm lying with healthy Arash. My head is resting on his hairy chest. His heartbeat is steady. He has both arms wrapped around my head, and he kisses me on my forehead. He strokes my hair while I close my eyes and go to sleep. I am safe. He is safe. I am protected. He is protected.

Chapter 10

The Scenic Route

Okay, so I'm driving through Colorado to Utah now. And when I arrive safely there, I check into my hotel. Richfield, Utah, is a small town off Interstate 70 in Utah. Next to my hotel was a gas station and a Wendy's. Across the street from my hotel was a strip of hotels and a few restaurants and bars. There really isn't much to do here. At least not for being in Richfield for one night. But that was okay, I was exhausted from the drive. I was driving and dancing. I was listening on that drive. I was wading through the ocean.

Utah also has a way of making you conscious of your thoughts as well. But I thought differently in Utah than I did in Colorado. Utah is where I experienced this internal battle while I passed the gas stations and actively decided not to listen to that voice and to continue driving. Utah is where I experienced the panic of being stranded in the desert with no gas and no phone to call for help. Utah is where I saw the ambulance and decided to follow it for those 40 miles on the way to the gas station. I was starting to think differently. I was changing my brain mechanisms. In Utah, there were a few places to stop along the highway labeled "Scenic View," where you could pull over and view the beauty of the mountains that you were driving through. These views are truly stunning. The views of the mountains look as if they could be a painting. You look out over these mountains, and you see the clouds almost resting peacefully on these mountains.

I have an internal battle while I passed this first sign for the scenic view. This was very similar to the one I faced when I passed those four gas stations in a row and consciously decided to listen to my ego and not His voice.

I am driving. I see this sign on the right: "Scenic View in 10 miles." I think to myself, should I stop? About an hour ago, I was extremely worried I was going to run out of gas on the side of the highway. I shouldn't stop. I need to get to my destination safe and sound. It's better to just get there at this point. I don't want to face that discomfort anymore. I want to be safe and sound in my hotel room. Reflecting on this, I was protecting my ego still. I've had a long day. I was tired. I needed to be safe. Again, I...I...I. My mind equaled being in my hotel room to being safe. However, that voice completely contradicts what my ego is telling me. It is quite literally telling me to do the exact opposite of what my ego is telling me to do.

So naturally, I choose my ego. I pass the first scenic view. I made a conscious decision not to listen to that voice. I know better. I am tired, I am hungry. I am ready to call it a day. I need to be safe. I, I, I. I didn't fully trust that I was safe following this voice yet.

But this time, it's different. I didn't experience that discomfort and anxiety that I did when I actively chose not to listen to the voice telling me to stop and get gas; this time, I actually felt bummed. Granted, I realize these are two completely different situations. But I felt like I was missing out. I was missing out on this beauty and wonder because my ego was still fragile and needed to be protected at all costs. But I have made the journey here, I had seen the complete beauty that was surrounding me while I drove through Illinois, Iowa, Nebraska, Colorado, and now Utah. I actually wanted to keep experiencing this beauty. My love for the beauty of this world and His work was greater than my fear of protecting my fragile ego from the trauma it had endured in the past few years.

This voice had inspired me. It ignited my passion for life. It opened my eyes.

I remember the pathway.

It's right over there.

Arash saw this path first, and he is right over there. He's safe.

A memory resurfaces.

When Arash passed—on Father's Day and Juneteenth—I had a dream that night. It is still so vivid in my memory. It is the only dream that I have had since Arash passed. It's the only dream where Arash visited me and spoke to me.

In this dream, Arash is wearing this purple and pink sweatshirt that I bought him for Christmas one year. I absolutely hated this sweatshirt. It was a running joke between Arash and I. He had sent me a link to this specific sweatshirt he wanted, and I resisted buying it for him because I thought it was too flashy, too colorful, too bold. But I ended up buying it for him for Christmas. And naturally, he wore it all the time.

I fell asleep the night Arash passed away. And Arash visits me in a dream wearing this pink and purple sweatshirt. He is dancing. He is laughing. He is completely healthy. He tells me, "Meg, I'm fine."

*****

Another memory resurfaces. During the last few weeks of Arash's life, we wanted to get Arash out of the house. He was on hospice and was at home too much. Arash is in a wheelchair at this point. Arya, Arash, Arya's girlfriend, Diya, and I went to a movie. I fell in love with going to the movies again that day. Such a simple concept. You go to the theater to watch a movie. You get popcorn to snack on, and for a few hours, you forget about the pain of the world. You forget about the trauma, evil, war, violence, and cancer that is in the world. But somehow, seeing this movie with Arash in a wheelchair made the movie better. That doesn't make sense. Everything around me is telling me that I should be depressed, worried, stressed, traumatized, upset, but I wasn't. I was filled with joy watching this movie with Arya and Arash. Arash was laughing throughout the movie, and he gave a thumbs-up. I had joy despite all circumstances.

*****

After passing that initial scenic-view sign, I am inspired by this voice. I was beginning to trust it. I was slowly beginning to listen to it. I reflected on everything that I had just gone through; I didn't think I was going to be okay when I first heard Arash's diagnosis. But I was okay. I don't understand why that happened. I don't understand why a twenty-six-year-old would be diagnosed with terminal brain cancer. I'm coming to terms with the fact that I will never understand that. But I'm not going to let this doubt hold me back anymore. I was going to stop at the next scenic view and take in that beauty. Something that Arash had been doing our entire relationship. I just hadn't seen it yet.

Chapter 11

Listening

Shannon and I went on a weekend trip to San Diego in June of 2023. I had been there once before with Arash and our friends Mitch and Maris back in July 2020. I fell in love with San Diego the first time I came here. When I visited with Shannon last year, I remembered this initial passion and fire this place ignites in me, and when we returned home to Chicago after that trip, I applied for my nursing license in California. I have a couple friends from nursing school that live in San Diego, and after talking to them and researching online, I discovered that it takes time to get this license. I submitted my application for this license on July 10, 2023, and received it on October 24, 2023. Reflecting on this, I think this was His voice telling me to apply for this license. And maybe the 3 months that I waited to get it approved was a wading period. Yes, I had other currents going on during this time. I was working for Misericordia and training for the marathon, but maybe this power that I heard in San Diego where I am passionate and listening was the positive pathway, the higher power, His voice.

After receiving this license, I always had the dream of moving to California in the back of my mind. But I wasn't ready to make a conscious decision to follow that voice quite yet. I continued doing what I knew. I continued working as a nurse at Misericordia. I continued following the Chicago marathon training schedule. I ran, I pray, I drove. I waded some more. I wasn't quite dancing yet. I faced the current of Misericordia, and I faced the current of running training.

Reflecting on this, why didn't I just listen? Why did it take me choosing my ego so many times to get to this point? Why did it cause me having multiple panic attacks and spiraling down a cycle of substance abuse to FINALLY listen? Again, I don't know. I'll never know. But I can remember my mom's words of wisdom: "Going through challenges and struggles in life makes you strong. It gives you character. You don't develop character or grit when life is going perfectly."

> Weather controls your day
> People make up your mind
> Until you can't even tell
> When someone gives you a sign
>
> But we make the ground our grave by layin' in it
> We make our problems fade by facin' 'em
> We make the wind our wings by raisin' your arms
> At the top of the world, yeah
>
> (Dominic Fike, "Dancing in the Courthouse")

Chapter 12

Flooding

I stopped at every scenic view after that. Without hesitation. I didn't even think about it. My ego was finally beginning to lose its power over me. I was willing to listen to His voice. I wanted to experience the beauty of this world, and I wanted to help others experience it and experience it with other people. In every circumstance and every situation.

Reflecting on this, I first opposed His voice because for some reason I thought I would be safer in the hotel room—my final destination for the day—than I would be stopping at this scenic view. I think that is because I'm familiar with hotels, I've been to many. I know what to expect. But stopping at the scenic route is unfamiliar to me. It's the unknown. It's unchartered territory. But I was safe in that moment. I wasn't going to be any safer than I was in that exact moment driving with Him than I would be stopping at the scenic route or arriving to my final destination. His voice is with you in every moment. He is the strength. He is the safety. This realization gives me joy and hope. You can appreciate each moment. You're safe with Him.

*****

After I subconsciously decide that I am no longer going to work at Misericordia anymore, I remember this voice that was still lingering in the back of my head about moving to California. I applied for that license back in July, and it's December, and I'm still thinking about this. It still inspires me. It motivates me. It excites me. It allows me to see hope, so I begin to apply for nursing jobs in San Diego. I think that if I get one of these jobs, then it's a sign I am meant to move here. If I don't get one of these jobs, then maybe it's my journey to stay put in Chicago. Again, I am trying to control the situation. I'll only listen if I get a job. If I have a clear sign, then I will listen and move to California. I am still depending on a job. I am still letting my ego win that battle that I know better than His voice. So weeks pass, I take a Zoom interview for an operating room in San Diego at my Chicago apartment. I don't get the job. I think, *Okay, this is a sign that I should stay here.* However, I continue to apply to nursing jobs in California. I continue to get emails saying, "Thank you for your application, but at this time, we have decided to go with another candidate..." I think, *Okay, this is another sign that I shouldn't listen and I should just stay in Chicago.* I receive even more emails. "Thank you for your application, but..."

Rejection. Rejection. Rejection.

At this point in my life, rejection is my middle name. I am used to rejection. This is nothing new for me. Rejection is my biggest motivator. These emails that I receive telling me NO don't even faze me because my ego is attached to the ship now. But still, I needed a SIGN that I should move to California. I needed some concrete proof that I was making the right decision here. I needed to feel safe in this decision. I was still letting my ego win the battle.

*****

I arrived safely in Utah. I check into my room. The hotel concierge is delightful.

For some reason, I am very conscious of the fact that Utah is a dry state. It really made me become conscious of my drinking. I had to think about it. The drive through Utah forced me to actually think about my drinking again. I came to a conclusion that I would actually be breaking the law if I repeated some of my drinking habits here that are legal in Chicago, Illinois.

So I'm aware now. I'm consciously aware that drinking is a universal issue. Trauma is a universal issue. War, violence, abuse, disease are universal problems. It's not just me that struggles with overcoming these traumas. The entire country has laws to try and prevent trauma from winning the battle. The entire world battles this trauma. I'm reminded that my ego and my story is but a drop in the infinity of the ocean. I find peace in this. I find peace in knowing I'm not alone.

*****

I take about two weeks after leaving Misericordia to relax and reflect. During this time, I prayed. I ran. I drove. I spent time with friends and family. Repetition is everything. Remember the pathway. I did not abuse alcohol. I consciously chose to dance through this waiting period. I am wading through the ocean peacefully. My anchor has been lifted; the trauma is now just a memory. My drinking has changed. Similar to loneliness, sometimes I get the urge to call up trauma for the night, but nah. I'm dancing up toward the ship now.

After taking a 40-day break from my coping mechanism and after changing my relationship with that coping mechanism, I feel like I can finally hear things clearly again. My brain doesn't have to work as hard to use the new *post* post-traumatic stress disorder mechanisms. It doesn't take as much energy to try and decipher what is the right next step and what is the wrong next step. This was no easy feat. I think the battle against the coping mechanism is almost as bad as the trauma itself. But there is beauty in this battle because you have learned to accept grace from this pathway, and now you can give yourself grace and other's grace and truly begin to enrich your life.

*****

I am laughing to myself in my tiny studio apartment as I hear a loud plane roaring above me about to land at the San Diego Airport. In the past, this loud noise would cause me extreme distress, but now,

I find comfort in the roaring of this plane. It makes me feel safe. I'm not alone.

*****

Arash is on this plane, about to go on his next trip. Yellow butterflies fill my studio apartment.

*****

Phew, I arrive in Utah. The plan is to spend a night in Richfield and drive to San Diego the following day. I receive phone calls from my father, my mother, and my grandparents warning me of the extreme flooding that was occurring in the Southern California region in the next few days. This includes San Diego. Gov. Gavin Newsom declared a state of emergency in eight heavily populated counties across Southern California. The storm included winds that gusted above one hundred miles per hour in some places and launched what National Weather Service described as "one of the most dramatic weather days in recent memory." The storm unleashed torrents of water across the state. Retaining walls collapsed, boulders and trees crashed down on roadways, mudslides damaged homes, and flash floods closed down portions of Interstate 5 and other major highways. Southern California residents were urged to stay at home and "only leave your house if it is absolutely necessary." The storm brought a swampy mess for millions of people who endured what was the "tenth wettest day in the history of the city dating back 150 years" (*The Washington Post*).

They are worried. The news is blaring with how extreme the flooding conditions are. My father advises that I (a) either stay a few nights in Utah until the flooding passes or (b) maybe drive halfway to California the following day and wait until the flooding passes there. That way, I'm closer to my final destination. Halfway to San Diego is about Las Vegas, Nevada. Sin City.

*****

So naturally, the internal war begins. What do I do? My ego is, of course, telling me that I am fine. I made it all the way here. I'm from Chicago. I've dealt with hazardous weather conditions the entire drive here and made it through. I got this. I'm going to drive to California! They don't know what they're talking about. I'm on a roll, and I'm not stopping now.

So I sit with this decision. Do I stay or do I go?

I use my new post-PTSD brain mechanisms.

Frist, I remember the pathway.

Second, I decipher which option is my ego's and which option is the higher power's voice.

This time, it's extremely easy to know which choice is following my selfish ego and which choice is following that peaceful pathway, that higher power, His voice.

Clearly, the right thing to do here is wait it out a few days. Either in Utah or Vegas.

But I decide to sleep on it and make that final decision in the morning. I only have the energy to worry about today at this point.

I have come to another realization at this point. This time, I am making this decision not for myself but for other people around me. Similar to how I was able to change my relationship with alcohol because I finally realized it wasn't about me anymore, it was about the people around me. I was changing my relationship with alcohol for them. I could only do this because of the peaceful pathway. The one that Arash saw first. My ego is telling me to keep my plan the same, wake up, and go to California. But now I am realizing that this decision does not only affect me, but it affects my mother, my father, and my grandparents, who all called me worrying about me. I love these people. I do not want to cause them anxiety or anguish. I consciously decide to disagree with my ego and follow the higher power's voice for the sake of people around me. I am joyfully and willingly making this decision. Similar to the pathway, California's not going anywhere. It'll always be there.

So what's the rush?

Chapter 13

Vegas, Part 1

I wake up in Utah the next morning. The extreme flooding is said to last a few days. So I have a choice to make: do I stay in Utah for a few nights, or do I drive halfway to Vegas, as my dad suggested?

First, pathway.

Second, I need to decipher which choice is my ego and which choice is the pathway's, the higher power's, His voice.

This time, I feel a shift in my ego. I am recognizing the change in my post-PTSD brain mechanisms. I have changed my relationship with alcohol. I do not abuse it anymore. I can have a drink or two, but I won't get too drunk because that would affect the other fish in the sea. We're all dancing and swimming to the top. I don't want to kill the vibe. So my ego is recognizing this and actually prefers to stay in Utah where the temptation of abusing alcohol in this dry state is less than in Las Vegas, the capital of temptation, Sin City.

*****

I love Las Vegas. It's one of my favorite cities in the world. I love the energy, I love the atmosphere. Anything goes here. Everyone is welcome. I love that beautiful Las Vegas strip. It fills your bones with anticipation for the night ahead of you. It's the big leagues for partying. It's a fun and vibrant place. The pools are stunning, the shows are fantastic, the food is terrific. You walk through the casinos, and you can see someone in pajamas on your left and someone in a ball gown or suit to your right. There's no rhyme or reason to Vegas. I love it.

I have been to Las Vegas multiple times for friends' birthdays, family vacations, and girls' trips. I've had the time of my life in Vegas on multiple occasions.

The last time I was in Las Vegas was with Arash. This was shortly after his brain cancer diagnosis. It was our last trip together. We, too, had a great time. We went out to great restaurants, we went to the new sports book that had just opened, we played blackjack and drank champagne in the casinos. We even went to the Chicago Bears versus Las Vegas Raiders game in the newly finished Allegiant Stadium.

*****

Reflecting on this, how blessed was I to have had these opportunities to experience this. Arash didn't have many years of life, but, boy, did he pack life into those years.

*****

I remember prior to that trip I was extremely anxious, worried, and scared. My ego was in survival mode. I hadn't seen the pathway yet. I was completely terrified to go to Las Vegas just Arash and I. He had just been diagnosed with brain cancer two months prior. What if he has a seizure on the plane? Or at the hotel? Or at the football game? What if his medications don't work? What if something horrible happens? These traumatic thoughts flooded my brain. However, Arash insisted we go. I know we got into an argument about this. I leaned on advice from my parents in regards of what to do and if I should go on this trip with him. They had mixed advice and opinions on this.

Ultimately, I decided to go. At the time, I was terrified. But looking back at it now as I sit in Mission Beach, California, I can confidently say that if I hadn't conquered that fear of going to Las

Vegas with Arash, not knowing how it would turn out, there is no way I would have had the courage to ultimately decide to go halfway to Las Vegas that day.

Arash was the one with brain cancer, and he wasn't afraid to go to Las Vegas on that trip. He had seen the pathway. I was on my way to seeing it.

*****

Arash is sitting across this bay in Mission Beach. He is smiling, but he tells me this is the last time he's going to talk to me from this point on. It'll be the pathway from now on. It's the higher power talking from now on. It's His voice now.

I say goodbye.

I'll see ya in eternity, Arash.

*****

The riptide of Mission Beach Bay is swaying perfectly to the left. They are calm. There are no big waves here. The riptide is moving in sync. I'm waiting to hear His voice again. I'm dancing with these waves. I'm enjoying the dancing, I'm enjoying the waiting period. That pathway is directly across the bay. It's standing perfectly still. Not going absolutely anywhere. I am confident in this. I'm conscious of His presence in this moment. It's going to be okay. We're all going to be okay. Keep your eye on the path and keep dancing. The sun is peeking from behind the clouds.

*****

Don't you worry,
Don't you worry, child
See Heaven's got a plan for you.
(Swedish House Mafia, "Don't You Worry
Child")

Chapter 14

Vegas, Part 2

So back to the daily internal war we all face every moment of every day.

I had a decision to make: do I stay in Utah for two days, or do I drive to Vegas and stay there for two days?

First, pathway.

Second, my ego has returned to survival mode. I forget about the ship for a little. (Quick! Pathway! Remember!) I was afraid to go to Vegas by myself. I have only gone there before with family, friends, or, most previously, Arash. Vegas is Sin City. There are temptations to abuse alcohol everywhere you turn. I know that I had changed my relationship with abusing alcohol. But did I really KNOW that? Or was that just a temporary state after a horrible, horrible night in December? Would I let this fear of being alone in Vegas be greater than my ability to NOT abuse alcohol? I was afraid to go to Vegas because I was afraid of what would win. Would I downward-spiral back into that horrible traumatic, self-loathing, inescapable cycle of trauma and alcohol abuse? This fear was amplified because I was alone. I was able to stop abusing alcohol because I had come to that realization I needed to stop abusing it for the sake of the people around me. But If I was going to Vegas alone, I didn't have that. It was just me versus my ego. And that is terrifying.

Trauma comes knocking. Absolutely not.

As my brother Brendan would say, "SHUT IT DOWNNNNNN!"

We are strong. We are past the PTSD. We are the war heroes now.

Bye, trauma! Forget you!

Well first, pathway.

Second, now that I have decided that my ego is in protective mode, this is different. This is no longer a fierce battle against the trauma anchor. Now this is a battle between my ego and the ship. Except this isn't a battle. We know the ship is good. We know this. The pathway! Arash saw it first! He was baptized! He was grasping that rosary for dear life on his last day. We KNOW this exists! So now this is a choice we have to make to TRUST the ship. The ship is good. It's peaceful. It's empowering. So let's choose to trust it.

Another new brain mechanism: we have to make a conscious decision to choose to trust the ship now. Trust the pathway. Trust the higher power. Trust the voice. Trust HIM. Trust Jesus!

From this point on, we are trusting what we know is true. That anchor is so far into the bottom of the sea it's a fragment of our imagination. Now we are looking directly into the pathway. Directly into that ship. We have no fear. We trust the voice. We trust him. And we're all in this together. Everybody. It's our mission now to follow this pathway and help others follow this pathway. We are dancing in sync with each other. And the pathway is good. The eternity waiting for us in this pathway is good.

> We're one but we're not the same
> We get to carry each other, carry each other
> One
> (U2 and Mary J. Blige, "One")

Now we are going to wake up every morning, it's easy now. This is so routine for us now. We got this.

Wake up, pathway.

Second, listen & decipher the voice.

Now, TRUST.

Okay, decision made. I'm going to Vegas for two days.

As my dear friend Laura would say, "Vegas, baby!"

Chapter 15

Vegas, Part 3

I decided to trust that morning, so I'm not driving to Vegas with the fear of my alcohol anchor. I'm driving with the trust I have in this badass ship. I'm extremely confident and blasting tunes the entire time to Vegas. The Super Bowl is next week in Vegas, so the city is going to be electric! I'm excited! Yellow butterflies everywhere!

Viva Las Vegas!

*****

Chicago Marathon: mile 21.

Shannon and I are running. We are exhausted. We are so tired. We can barely speak to each other. We need to conserve all our energy to get through these next few miles. We look to the crowd and see our family and friends cheering us on. This gives us an absolute jolt of energy. We are inspired by them! We are now not doing this for ourselves but for them! They cheered us on, so we can do this!

Vegas: Night 1

Once I arrived to Vegas and checked into my hotel room for the next two nights, I face the next challenge: Okay, California is the destination. But you're in limbo for two days because of the extreme flooding there. This is out of your control. It's simple. We don't worry about things we can't control anymore. So we won't even waste time worrying about that.

We will face the next challenge: boredom. I am sitting in my hotel room facing the question "What do I DO now?" Similar to the question I asked after Arash passed away.

You're in boredom. Limbo. You're wading in the water. But we already know that we choose to dance when we're bored. So what do we do?

First, pathway.

Second, decipher His voice.

Okay...this is a little trickier. I'm in Las Vegas. There are really two extremes here. To go out and booze, gamble, and party OR to stay in my hotel room and get a good night's sleep for the next day.

Or is there a middle ground?

I'm going to sit with this for a little bit. Again, there's extreme flooding in California. The weather is out of our control. There is no rush.

I'm going to break this down.

What is His voice telling me to do?

I listen. I wade. I dance. But I don't really hear anything. I'm also alone.

But I'm not really alone. Because the pathway is right over there. We know this. We're never ACTUALLY alone.

I am realizing now that I had not had a drink since December 21st after that horrible night. I haven't had a sip of liquor. It is now February 5th. I haven't had a sip of alcohol in 47 days. Now I am in Las Vegas. A place that is literally named Sin City. Alcohol is everywhere. I'm not alone. But I don't have friends or family here to NOT abuse alcohol for. So…

My dad calls me. I told him that I decided to go to Las Vegas. My dad also loves Las Vegas, and he too has not had a drink in 47 days since that horrible night. I ask for his advice as to what to do now that I'm here.

I can hear the excitement in his voice. He is more excited that I'm in Vegas than I am!

"Oh, Meg, you have to go to a show or have a drink at a sports book or something!"

This completely contradicts with Mom's advice: "Stay in the hotel room and push a chair against the door and dead bolt it!" I'm chuckling as I write this.

So I think. Thanks for the advice, guys! This doesn't help me at all.

It's the same dilemma that I was facing before I spoke with them on the phone.

So, pathway.

Listen & decipher.

A memory resurfaces. When Arash and I were in Las Vegas, we went to a magic show one night. And I remember that I only had a drink or two because I couldn't get drunk. Arash has brain cancer. I have to be on my toes in case something happens. I remember that purpose: I had to be coherent and functioning for him as he had been for me prior to being diagnosed with cancer.

So I think the voice is maybe telling me to step out of my comfort zone and go to a show alone. This could be an opportunity to experience something new. I have never gone to a comedy show by myself before. I mean, I am in Vegas, for God's sake!

*****

Arash was always going to shows, concerts, games, any type of event where he could experience the beauty and wonder of this world! Now, I understand why.

*****

Okay, now, is the real decision I have to make: Do I get a drink? Do I willingly put myself in a situation where I am face-to-face with the trauma that I have successfully avoided for 47 days? Do I willingly go to war with alcohol? Do I willingly battle the trauma that has been passed down for generations and generations before me? The trauma that existed way before I was born? The trauma that caused families to move to new places for better lives to avoid this trauma?

First, pathway.

Second, listen & decipher.

My ego's initial first thought is, *HELL NO! Look at how far you've come. There is no way you're going to spiral down. You are not strong enough to fight this level and depth of trauma. No way. Don't even think about it.*

But then I remember that memory with Arash at the magic show. I remember that I only had 1-2 drinks and was coherent. I actually was coherent the whole weekend. I didn't get wasted. I had a reason NOT to drink. Arash was sick. That happened. That was real. In that moment, I made a conscious decision to NOT abuse alcohol but to drink it responsibly. And when I reflect on this, I am realizing that this was the same brain mechanism as the one I'm trying to train my brain to remember. This brain mechanism was morphed by PTSD. But we are now post-PTSD. I was able to stop abusing alcohol for 47 days because I had finally come to the realization that it was affecting the other people around me. I had finally gotten out of my own head and my own ego. My ego of self is slowly being morphed into a ship. So this gives me the confidence. Maybe I can have a drink or two and not abuse it. I've done it in the past.

Still, I'm not entirely sure what the right move here is. I'm still unsure of what He is trying to tell me, and even while I'm writing this, I'm struggling to completely decipher his voice. Like I said, this was and still is the most challenging battle after Arash passed. This is not going to happen overnight. My brain is still recovering from years of abusing alcohol and trauma.

So I'm going to keep listening and dancing.

*****

I'm finding that when I am having difficulty deciphering His voice, it helps to distract myself. For example, I'll go on a run or change what room I'm in or go somewhere. Just change your perspective. Anything. You could literally walk from the bedroom to the kitchen. Just distract yourself when you're listening and don't hear anything. Don't try to force it. As you have read, I had been doing that for years. It doesn't work.

So I'll go on a run, or go listen to music, or go outdoors. Nature is great. Just don't stay in the same spot for too long. You have to keep dancing and wading. We already decided that we are looking at boredom as dancing now, boredom is NOT sitting still. Because if you sit still for too long, that anchor's going to get you.

*****

Arash loved to travel, we never sat still. Now, I understand why.

*****

Okay, so I was able to have 1-2 drinks with Arash at that comedy show. The real question is: can I do that again? Can I drink alcohol without abusing it? I reflect on what my motivator was when I drank 1-2 drinks with Arash. It was fear. I was afraid to get too drunk because my fear of the worst-case scenario with Arash's brain cancer was greater. So essentially, the worst-case scenario was death. I was afraid of death.

*****

A memory resurfaces. I had a really genuine friend after Arash passed away. We were in similar currents at the time. We spent an entire summer together. You really see people's true colors going through trauma. I really hope he's doing well. He was a genuine soul who truly deserves the best in life.

*****

Again, listening & dancing.

*****

Okay, I was afraid of death. Essentially. Arash, who had come face-to-face with death prior to this diagnosis, wasn't afraid of death. He was the one who wanted to go to Vegas.

*****

After this entire journey, I can confidently say I'm not afraid of death anymore.

*****

When I die and they lay me to rest
Gonna go to the place that's the best
When I lay me down to die
Goin' up to the spirit in the sky
(Norman Greenbaum, "Spirit in the Sky")

*****

Confidently, I'm not afraid of death anymore. We have conquered this anchor. Actually, He conquered this anchor. He showed us that this anchor becomes a ship. Arash saw this first. He was baptized. He was grasping that rosary where Jesus is dying on the cross in the last moments of life. He could not talk, he could not walk, he could not speak. But he grasped onto that rosary with all his strength. Until the very end. But Arash himself did not conquer this anchor, Jesus did.

*****

So you know what? My faith and trust in the ship is greater than my fear of death. We KNOW this is true. The pathway! It's sitting right over there. It was sitting there when Arash had his last breath, and it's been there ever since.

Now that I see this pathway, now that I sat at the bay in Mission Beach, California, and see this pathway across the bay, the pathway is the sun shining, it's the palm trees surrounding you, it's the beautiful body of water in front of you with a pleasant riptide passing you by. This is the pathway now.

So when I think of the pathway now, I'm going to consciously choose to think of this pathway. The pathway full of life. I will consciously pick this pathway over the initial one I saw when Arash was dying. I will choose the pathway of life over death.

*****

Arash told me this is the correct path. And that now it was time for him to go.

Now I'm following that higher power's voice, His voice. Jesus's voice.

*****

When the sun had left and the winter came
And the sky fall could only bring the rain
I sat in darkness, all broken hearted
I couldn't find a day I didn't feel alone
I never meant to cry, started losing hope
But somehow baby, you broke through and saved
me

You're an angel, tell me you're never leaving
Cause you're the first thing I know I can believe
in
You're holy, holy, holy, holy
I'm high on loving you, high on loving you
You're holy, holy, holy, holy
I'm high on loving you, high on loving you

(Florida Georgia Line, "H.O.L.Y.")

*****

I want to run, I want to hide
I wanna tear down the walls that hold me inside
I wanna reach out and touch the flame
Where the streets have no name, ha, ha, ha
I wanna feel sunlight on my face
I see that dust cloud disappear without a trace
I wanna take shelter from the poison rain
Where the streets have no name, oh, oh
Where the streets have no name
Where the streets have no name
We're still building then burning down love
Burning down love
And when I go there, I go there with you
It's all I can do
(U2, "Where the Streets Have No Name")

*****

Okay, I now have to train my brain to think like this daily. This will be a daily choice.

New routine:

First, Pathway of Life. NOT death.

Second, Listen & decipher.

Third, TRUST.

*****

Okay, back to Vegas. Do I have a drink at the comedy show or not?

First, pathway of Life. NOT death.

Second, listen & decipher.

Third, trust.

But now that we are looking at this after seeing the new pathway at Mission Beach that is filled with sun and palm trees and perfectly moving riptides. We can make decisions knowing that this is the correct pathway. Of life.

So I am going to try to have a drink or two tonight and see how I handle it.

I trust Him now after seeing this. & I am going to drink in a different way now. I am confident I can do this.

> With Man, this is impossible, but with God
> all things are possible. Matthew 19:26

*****

I get ready and go to dinner at the Rio before the comedy show. I order one vodka soda lime, always my drink of choice. I take a sip. This time, I do feel different.

First, pathway of *life*.

Second, listen & decipher.

Third, *trust*.

This time is different because this time, I KNOW that the positive pathway of life is with me while I drink this vodka soda. It's sitting with me at this table. It's always present. It's always good. It's always life giving. I am recognizing that this is a post-PTSD brain mechanism. Again, I know that this is something I need to practice every day. It's not going to happen overnight, & it will be a choice that I need to consciously make every day until I finally enter that life giving pathway.

Before, I didn't think the pathway was with me when I was drinking alcohol. Now, I know it is.

*****

So I take a sip of this drink, and I start to dance. I don't want to get too drunk, I want to be in sync with this vibe. I don't want to mess up the dancing of other people in the sea. I'm vibing. I'm enjoying the wading, I've turned boredom into dancing. Well, really, He has. I am now drinking for the celebration of the pathway. It's no longer done in fear of the traumatic pathway.

*****

I finish this drink, and I feel good about this. I am enjoying drinking with this new perspective. I can sip on a drink while I'm dancing in the ocean with the other people on our way to the top. We're vibing.

*****

Yeah, do you believe in magic?
Yeah, believe in magic of the young girl's soul
Believe in the magic of a rock 'n' roll
Believe in the magic that can set you free
Ahh, talking 'bout the magic
(The Lovin' Spoonful, "Do You Believe in Magic")

*****

After dinner, I go to the comedy show at the Rio. As I enter, there is a bar to my right.

Can I get one more? I am in Vegas, for God's sake!

First, pathway of *life*.

Second, listen & decipher.

Third, *trust*.

The pathway is good. He is good. Life is good. I can have one more drink, but that's it! I wouldn't want to get any more drinks once the show starts because that would disrupt the flow of the comedy show. I don't want to get too drunk & mess up the dance! I don't want to mess up the vibe or affect anyone else's dance.

I want to enjoy this new experience and learn something from each comedian.

*****

> I don't wanna look at anything else now
> that I saw you
> I don't wanna think of anything else now
> that I thought of you
> I've been sleeping' so long in a twenty-year
> dark night
> And now I see daylight, I only see daylight
> (Taylor Swift, "Daylight")

*****

I take an Uber home and arrive back to the hotel room.

*****

When I reflect on my history of alcohol abuse, I am trying to decipher what the difference was between the drinking I did while Arash was sick and after he passed. I've already realized that I was able to control my drinking while Arash was sick because I had a

203

reason *not* to drink. People were depending on me. I had to control my drinking for them.

But after Arash passed, my drinking completely downward spiraled. Why is that?

For four years, I would come home at the end of the night to Arash. For four years, I was not alone at the end of the night. Arash was next to me. But now that Arash had passed, I was going home at the end of the night to no one. Just myself and my old friend loneliness.

But now that I am training my brain to think differently because I am post-PTSD now. I'm going to think about this decision on my way home from the Rio to my hotel room, where I will be alone. This is always the hardest part of the day when you perceive that you're alone, nighttime.

First, pathway of life. I know that I am not alone anymore. The pathway of life is with me.

Second, listen & decipher. I'm listening for His direction. I'm waiting and dancing. I don't want to be out of sync with the riptide of the ocean. I'm vibing to the rhythm of that song that is playing from the ship at the top of the shore. I'll call up my friend freedom for the night. I lost my old friend loneliness's phone number. So that's no longer an option.

Third, *trust*. This is the beginning of this new life. I just saw the pathway of life yesterday, so each day is new and full of opportunities to experience the beauty and wonder of life. Each day is an opportunity to learn from the people around you. This is awesome!

So when I finally arrive back to my hotel room and I'm lying in bed with my ego, I am focusing on the ship. I am choosing to focus on the positive experience of that day. I am reflecting on the beauty of Vegas. I am reflecting on the delicious food. I am reflecting on the stories the comedians told. I feel my mind start to ease and drift to sleep because I can find peace in knowing that when I wake up tomorrow, that pathway of life will be there waiting for me. My best friend sitting at the trunk of the tree will be waiting for me.

*****

Vegas, Day 2

I wake up in Vegas.

First, pathway of life.

Second, listen & decipher. I did it! I only had two drinks! I didn't get into an extremely bad fight with my boyfriend. No one around me got arrested! No more trauma! I went to a great dinner and saw a great show!

Third, TRUST.

Again, repetition is everything. I pray, & I run today. Evening comes, and the question of "What do I *do*?" returns.

Okay, last night I was able to have 1 drink at dinner and 1 drink at the comedy show. I know the pathway is with me, but essentially, I was by myself.

So tonight I am listening to His voice to grow and experience more beauty and wonder. I am listening to His voice to not stay cooped up in my hotel room for the night because He conquered fear. So to choose to stay in my hotel room out of fear would be a waste of time and pointless. This would actually inhibit my learning and growth.

I am moving to a new city tomorrow. I need to learn how to meet new people and expand my horizons. So I chose to trust him and get a drink at the casino bar. Only one though because I have a long drive tomorrow!

*****

I get to the bar, and an older man approaches me and strikes up a conversation. I am by myself (Well, not really). But this does create some anxiety and tension. Yesterday, I went out, but I didn't really interact with any new people. It was just me. But again, I'm moving to a new city. I need to get used to this. I need to embrace this. I need to grow and learn from all experiences in life.

So I begin speaking with this man.

*****

Reflecting on my history of substance abuse, I think one of the things that also caused me to drink so much and abuse alcohol was how much I cared what everyone thought of me. I was a people pleaser. Before I saw this pathway, I was just wading in the ocean, swimming from current to current, trying to find a foundation that simply doesn't exist in this current. Foundation does not exist in the thoughts, perceptions, or opinions of other people. Foundation only occurs in the pathway. In the ship. In Him. In Life. I wanted to be perceived as being fun, and I genuinely wanted people around me to have fun. So instead of focusing on the pathway to make decisions, I focused on the people around me to make decisions.

So if I was interacting with someone, I would respond in the way that I perceived they would want me to. I would think of the current before the path. I hadn't seen the path yet. This simply is just not sustainable for life. You can only do this for so long before that anchor gets you.

I had a lot of anxiety in school, a lot of anxiety going to work, a lot of anxiety going to social events, and just a lot of anxiety in general because of this intense need to please everyone. I had no ship. For some reason, I thought alcohol would help with this anxiety. We know that anxiety is a trauma now. & trauma has been defeated. This is old news to us. We have the path of life now. So to dwell on the past is pointless and a waste of time.

*****

I'm reflecting on the differences between the types of anxiety I experienced on my drive to California. The first, when I was driving past the gas stations in Utah consciously deciding not to listen to His voice and the second when I consciously decided not to listen to His voice and stop at the scenic routes. Anxiety really just occurs when you're consciously deciding to not listen to Him.

When I was at parties in college, I hadn't seen the path. So I only had my ego. We know that listening to your ego and not listening to His voice causes contradiction in our brains, leading to physical and/or mental discomfort (a.k.a. panic attacks a.k.a. anxiety?).

I hadn't seen the path, so I didn't know what was causing my anxiety. But now I have. And if we know the cause of something, we can work to fix it.

Again, anxiety has been defeated. So to dwell on the past is pointless and a waste of time. I'm reminding myself of that as I write this right now. Kick that trauma to the ground. We're on the verge of being pros at this point.

So when I passed that gas station in Utah and didn't listen to Him, this created anxiety. But my anxiety was lifted when I saw that ambulance and followed it to the gas station. Maybe that was the moment, that this anxiety, this trauma, that each and every one of us faces daily turned from death to life. What once triggered PTSD now I could look at and find peace. Because we know the pathway is life, not death.

*****

The next time I faced anxiety after this moment was when I didn't listen to His voice telling me to stop at that scenic view in Utah. This was a completely different kind of anxiety than previously. This was anxiety that was fueled by my subconscious desire to follow His voice. Subconsciously, I wanted to stop and see the beauty. But my conscious wasn't aware of that yet. My conscious still saw the motivator as fear. Again, this transformation just happened. It's us post-PTSD. It's new. It's unchartered territory. But it's life-giving unchartered territory. It's following the path of life. The motivator is now life.

So now we can make a conscious decision that when we inevitably listen to our precious, fragile egos over Him, we can recognize that this is human nature, but now we can make a conscious decision to pick the scenic route.

*****

Ok, so back to Vegas.

I'm sitting at the bar in Vegas when an older man comes up to me at the bar. My brain mechanisms have changed. This is the post PTSD, willingly listening, willingly dancing towards the top of the ocean, willingly following the pathway-of-life brain.

First, life.

Second, listen & decipher.

Third, trust.

Fourth, pick life again.

*****

My ego is confident and is telling me to have another drink or two or three... See where the night takes you. His voice speaks very clearly to me. The plan was to have one drink, you're going to California tomorrow!

I trust this. I have one drink. I don't want to get too drunk and disturb the current at this bar. I don't want to disturb the other people at this bar's vibe. I am waiting, I am vibing, I am dancing. I am following the rhythm of that song on the ship. I am learning from this new experience; I am growing from this new experience. I'm listening to the performers at the Piano Bar at Harrah's. I'm vibing to the song. I'm part of this current. I'm enjoying this experience.

When I return home to my hotel room, I'm calling freedom up tonight.

California, baby!

*****

Chicago Marathon: Mile 22.

Shannon and I are completely exhausted. We are running solely with our hearts at this point. Alone, our physical and mental abilities are not capable of finishing this race. We need to look deeper, we need to look up toward the ship. Only a few more miles to go! We can do this!

Chapter 16

Inspiration

The drive from Las Vegas to California…Wow. I cannot emphasize how beautiful this was. I felt like I was driving through the winding hills during the beginning credits of a movie. I felt the magic as I drove across the state line. "Welcome to California!" I took my time with this drive; I took the scenic route. The music is on, and I am ready to arrive at my destination. The sun is shining, the sky is the brightest blue I've ever seen, and the white clouds are perfectly still. Excitement fills my bones. I can feel hope flowing in my bloodstream. I am passionate. I am motivated. I am inspired. I am driving toward that ship. And no trauma, no anchor can hold me back. We are completely past that. We are in this together. We don't have to fear. We have each other to lean on when storms come our way. We have a foundation that cannot be shaken. It cannot be taken away from us. Regardless of what happens when we arrive to California, that foundation is solid. It's not going absolutely anywhere. So we can be confident on this drive to California, we can do anything! We can change the world.

*****

A memory resurfaces. Before I left Chicago to make the road trip to California, I had to pack my belongings and clean out my closet at my apartment in Chicago. The last article of clothing that I had of Arash's was his pink-and-purple sweatshirt. At this point, I had donated or thrown out all his other belongings because it was too painful to hold on to them. But this sweatshirt I could not throw away. It made me laugh; it made me smile. It reminded me of the dream I had the night he passed. I couldn't give this away.

But the day before I left on this trip, I stopped at Good Will to drop off this sweatshirt. What once would have broken my heart now filled my heart with joy.

*****

After about a solid four to five days on the road, I finally arrived at San Diego, California, and checked into my tiny studio Airbnb apartment. I am still under the illusion that I can afford to live in San Diego. Ha!

*****

Just because we made it here does not mean that our work is done. We're still not ready to take that last breath at the top of the ocean. There is too much beauty, there is too much wonder still out there. There are too many currents to swim through and learn and grow from. I do not want to choose the path of death; I want to choose the path of life every morning. The anchor is lifted, and now there is the ship.

So the first day that I wake up in California, I face the same challenges, the same struggles, the same internal battle that I have been facing all along. Just because we made it here doesn't mean that the trauma doesn't exist. Yes, he defeated it, so we can defeat it daily now. But it's not going to be easy. We saw Arash's journey. This wasn't easy. But it was worth it. Arash is now in a peaceful eternity past Mission Bay Beach, where the sun is shining, the palm trees are standing perfectly still, and the riptide is moving in perfect rhythm. But we're not there yet.

So the question resurfaces: what do we *do*?

*****

I had taken a huge leap of faith here. I drove to California with no job. I had paid for an Airbnb for two months while I still had to pay my rent on my Chicago apartment.

Yikes! Even writing this, I'm a little unsure if this was the most logistically smart move.

Pathway! Quick!

But when I look at the pathway in all its pain and trauma now turned to grace and hope, I am instantly put at ease. My foundation lies in something that my career, my relationships, my bank account, my shelter can never give me: Him.

So first, life.

Second, listen & decipher.

Third, trust.

Fourth, pick life again.

I've had a lot of time to reflect since arriving in California. I've explored the beautiful beaches, I've frequented Balboa Park, I've traveled to the different neighborhoods in San Diego and gone to new restaurants and new bars. I've met new people, and I've enjoyed the sunshine.

I'm listening now.

What do I *do*?

The question I asked myself when Arash passed away, the question I asked myself after I left Elmhurst Hospital, after I left

Northwestern Hospital, after I left Misericordia. The question that I asked myself at the beginning of every day on my road trip here.

As I sit in my tiny studio apartment in San Diego, I'm accepting that this question isn't going anywhere. In fact, this question has been His voice all along. It has been present my entire life. I just was never able to fully decipher it. I had just never sat face-to-face with it. I used to be afraid of it.

For so long, I was listening to my ego answering this question. I was answering the question in terms of the anchor. But now I'm listening. Now I'm listening to the ship's voice for the answer to that question.

I recognize that this isn't easy. I recognize that this will be a daily battle. It will go against my ego. But we know that our egos are transforming to ships, anyway.

*****

Back to the interview, where I completely bombed the first question. Like, royally bombed this question. Like the interviewers could have asked me, "Do you even know what job you're applying to?" and kindly ended the interview in that moment.

I'm going to break this down again. Like I said, I'm still frolicking around California and have a lot of time to think here. The pathway is nudging me that it may be time to get a job and start contributing to society again! LOL!

First, *life*. Always.

Second, listen & decipher.

Third, *trust*.

Fourth, *life*. *Again*.

I am basically starting fresh in a new city. I don't really know anyone here. I don't know much about San Diego. Or nursing in San Diego. And I recognize that. Of course, I've done research on the different hospitals in the area. I've talked to my friends here about their experiences at the hospitals they work in and learned from their experiences in San Diego. I'm recognizing that I myself really don't know too much about San Diego.

Yikes! Can I still move back to Chicago?

Quick! Pathway!

But you know what, that's okay. I have been doing my best to follow that pathway, that voice, that higher power, and it's led me here.

So wherever you're at, just take a deep breath. Give yourself some grace. You're exactly where you're supposed to be.

I am recognizing all the mistakes I've made along the way, and I'm forgiving myself quicker than I did when I was tied to the anchor. Arash would want me to. He would want me to.

But where do you go from here? Essentially from square one?

You can't completely forget about the anchor. I mean, it's a part of you. It's actually a very important part of you. It's what allowed you to see the ship. We don't have to look at this negatively anymore. Without the anchor, without the actual trauma, without the actual breaking point, without the actual death, you'd still have no foundation. You'd still be in that infinite ocean living for the approval of others and swimming from current to current with no real strength, no real direction, no real grit, no real character. The anchor gave you that.

So I'm going to take a moment and just be thankful for that.

*****

The first week that I arrived in San Diego, I applied for multiple nursing jobs online. Again, I'm still under the illusion that I can afford to live here, and I can't live off microwave popcorn forever!

I even considered applying to jobs that weren't nursing. I'm in California, I can be whoever I want. I can do whatever I want. If I truly want to start over, this is the time and the place to do it. The world is my oyster. I drove thirty hours to California. I can do anything.

But careful, this ego-over-ship thinking is what caused that rope to engulf your ankle.

So now when I get the urge to call my old friend ego for the day, I'm going to remember how deep that water can get when you're tied to the anchor.

*****

> When you go through deep waters, I will be with you. When you go through rivers of difficulty, you will not drown. When you walk through the fire of oppression, you will not be burned up; the flames will not consume you. For I am the LORD, your God, the Holy One of Israel, your Savior. (Isaiah 43:2–3)

*****

So instead, I'm going to call up my new friend lifeguard. He's new. He's cute. He's fun. And he'll keep you safe. He's not going to let me go too far into that water.

*****

So I try to listen and decipher which voice is my ego and which voice is His.

The waiting period, my old friend. I've been so busy with the road trip here and moving in and just adjusting to this new place that I haven't really just sat in this waiting period yet. I've been keeping myself busy with exploring new places and meeting new people. But that pathway of life has led me here once again. The waiting period. The wading in the ocean. I can leave Elmhurst, I can leave Northwestern, I can leave Misericordia, I can even leave Chicago. But that waiting period isn't going anywhere. It will catch up with you. You can distract yourself in many new and exciting currents. And this is great! But ultimately, it'll bring you back to that still riptide in front of the pathway of life and remind you of His bigger picture. His pathway. His plan.

But now we are thankful for this waiting period, this riptide, the boredom that we have turned to dancing. This waiting period is the safety net that your good friend lifeguard has thrown to you. He's new. He's cute. He'll protect you and keep you safe.

*****

Follow Me, and I will make you fishers of men. (Matthew 4:19)

*****

Today is a cloudy, rainy day in San Diego. But I like going to the beach when it's cloudy. It's nice to take a break from the sun. It's nice to sit on the beach in a sweatshirt and leggings. Your toes are still sinking into the sand, and even though the sun isn't shining, you can still look out over the ocean and see infinity. The ships are still there even if the sun isn't shining, and the drizzle is coming down. It's peaceful.

I'm sitting on Coronado Beach in my favorite bright red Chicago Bulls sweatshirt. I first bought this sweatshirt when we went to the Chicago Bulls game for Arash's birthday, Halloween. This was two months after he was diagnosed with brain cancer. We had a great time at the game. Our seats were in the nosebleeds, but we didn't care, we were just happy to be there. It didn't matter where our seats were, it didn't matter if they won the game or lost the game (I know Arash would disagree with this because he inevitably had multiple bets on the game), but we were just happy. Arash had brain cancer, but we were still happy. We still went to a Bulls game. We had fun.

This memory kind of reminds me of sitting on the beach on a cloudy, rainy day. I can still enjoy this. I can still see the positive pathway across the ocean. I can still see that ship. I can still feel the higher power's presence, His presence. It doesn't matter if the sun isn't out. It doesn't matter if I'm a little uncomfortable because of the drizzle or the chill. I can still enjoy it. The ship is unchanging. It withstands the test of trials, tribulations, trauma.

I used to wear this sweatshirt to Northwestern all the time. Arash had a few stays in the hospital for his seizures.

*****

I remember sitting at the Perri's house one morning with Arash, his parents, and Arya while we were drinking coffee and eating croissants while watching *Good Morning America*. This was always on at the Perris' house. Every morning. It was comforting. Arash was very sick at this point. He had very little mobility, and he couldn't communicate besides giving us a thumbs-up. I remember that my mother and my aunt Sue were going to visit Shannon at the University of Illinois for Mom's Weekend, and they invited me to come with.

I remember being torn on what to do. On one hand, I wanted to stay at home with Arash. He was so sick at this point I wanted to make sure I could still be there for him and help with his care. I felt like going to U of I to party with my mom and sister would have been an extremely selfish decision, and I would hate myself if something happened while I left. I will never forget the kindness the Perris showed to me when making that decision. They encouraged me to go. They wanted me to still have joy and have fun. And to continue living. "Arash would want you to." And I'm realizing how true that statement was. Even when Arash was sick, he continued to go to Bulls games, see friends, attend family parties, and travel to Vegas. He didn't allow that fear, that trauma, that anchor to prevent him from still enjoying the beauty and wonder of life.

So I went. And we had an absolute blast.

Two days later, when we were checking out of the hotel and getting ready to say goodbye to Shannon and to make the drive back to Chicago, I receive a text from Arya that Arash was in the emergency room at Northwestern. He had a seizure that wouldn't stop.

*****

I remember that drive very vividly. My mom, my aunt Sue, and I drove from Champaign, Illinois, to Chicago, Illinois. We didn't speak too much. We were all worried for Arash. I remember that we played music the entire time and how healing and helpful this was. I grasped onto that music like it was my life buoy in the ocean. I meditated on the words. I could feel the rhythm of each song in my bones as I looked out the window and saw the rolling meadows of the farmland. I felt like I was transported to the funeral procession driving to the cemetery completely alone while I look out my window and see the rest of the world standing still. I felt completely helpless. There was absolutely nothing I could do to help this situation. I think that's when I first became extremely conscious that there is a higher power and a bigger plan. I am but a drop in the ocean. His plan is way bigger than mine. It was way bigger than the Perri's. It was completely incomprehensible. I could try all I wanted to control this situation. But there is simply nothing I could do. There's nothing any of us could do. This was way bigger than us and our precious, fragile egos. At the time, this caused me sorrow and pain. But looking at it now, it causes me to feel free.

*****

I arrived back to Chicago and went to Northwestern to see Arash and the Perri's. I don't remember the details of that hospital stay. But I do remember noticing that out the window of his hospital room I could see a large office building stretching up into the sky and behind that I could see Lake Michigan.

That pathway, that higher power, that voice, that ship, that life, that infinity, Him. It was there the entire time.

*****

Mmm, baby I don't understand this
You're changing, I can't stand it
My heart can't take this damage
And the way I feel, I can't stand it
Mmm, baby, I don't understand this
You're changing, and I can't stand it
My heart can't take this damage
And the way I feel, can't stand it

Mmm, baby, I don't understand it
(XXXTentacion, "Changes")

*****

Sometimes when I feel the trauma or anxiety slowly surfacing back up, I have to make an emergency phone call to my friend the lifeguard. I have to do this immediately so that rope doesn't grasp my ankle.

9-1-1.

My cute new friend lifeguard throws me a life buoy, and this life buoy has a word written on it: *Distract*.

When a memory creeps into your thoughts…when you feel that anxiety beginning to build up…when you feel the rope slowly grasping your ankle…when you can hear trauma whispering your name at the bottom of the ocean…

You need to react. QUICK. Except this is an emergency phone call to 911. You don't have time to sit with your thoughts in the waiting period to really think and decipher.

So you call 911, and the lifeguard throws you a life buoy with the word *Distract*. Yes, sir. We're on it.

Change your location, change your perspective. Immediately. Listen to music. Go on a run. Read a book. Go outside. It can be as simple as walking from one end side of the street to the other. Keep moving. Do not sit still.

*****

I think that's one of the reasons I love Balboa Park so much. There's so many different little coves here. Right now I am sitting at a table next to the San Diego Museum of Art, but across the way is a craft café, and to my left is a pathway to a completely different part of this park that I haven't even seen yet. There are numerous opportunities for exploration and growth everywhere I turn. But that is universal. Exploration and growth is anywhere you're at. Just keep your eye on the ship, and follow that voice's direction.

*****

Yeah, God's taking care of the weather (woo)
Life don't get much better
Than ice in a cup, a cup on my lips
Steal another kiss and take another sip
Of tequila on a boat

Yeah, time's moving real slow
Drop that anchor down out in the middle
Everybody, drink a little
(Dustin Lynch, "Tequila on a Boat")

*****

Sorry, I digress! Back to the Chicago Bulls sweatshirt.

I distinctly remember wearing this Chicago Bulls sweatshirt to Northwestern on multiple occasions. When I was living at home while Arash was sick, I would wake up every morning. I would run, eat a healthy breakfast, and then go to Northwestern to be with Arash and his family.

One hospital visit, Arash had to stay a few nights in the hospital to get his seizures under control. I remember during this hospital stay, multiple family members, cousins, and friends would come to visit Arash. His friends would sit with the Perri's and me and exchange funny stories about Arash growing up and the good memories they all shared.

There it is again, that sense of community. That sense of dependability. Their presence was power. Their presence was strength. Without his family and friends coming to visit, there is no way we would have been able to get through those long hospital stays.

Arash could not talk, walk, or speak at this time, and his friends still showed up to see him in the hospital. Every single time. Without a doubt. No matter what.

*****

I also wore this Chicago Bulls sweatshirt the night that Arash was admitted to an inpatient hospice facility for a night following multiple seizures at home and an ambulance ride to JourneyCare.

There was a Bulls game on that night, and Arash's cousins and friends showed up to the hospice facility that night to sit in his hospital room and watch the game. I will never forget the importance of their presence.

Again, Arash could not talk, he could not walk, and he could not speak. His friends still showed up to see him at this facility. Every single time. No matter what. I specifically remember that there were strict visitor restrictions at this time due to the COVID-19 facilities, but the hospice nurses were so kind as to let us break these rules so 12 of Arash's closest friends could come over and watch the Bulls game.

*****

I'm sitting in Balboa Park as I write this wearing that Chicago Bulls sweatshirt. What once would have brought me traumatic memories now brings me a sense of security and comfort in remembering this strong sense of community.

In fact, it's pretty chilly out here today. I might have to put my LA Lakers sweatshirt on over it.

But the chilliness is starting to creep in, so I might have to just switch to the other side of the table where the sun's at.

*****

Chicago Marathon: Mile 23.

Shannon's phone just ran out of battery. She can't listen to music through her AirPods anymore. Now we are both listening to music that is playing out loud on my phone. We're listening to the Spotify playlist that my brother Brendan made for us. Only a few more to go.

> We all have a hunger (we all have a hunger)
> We all have a hunger (we all have a hunger)
> We all have a hunger (we all have a hunger)
> We all have a hunger (we all have a hunger)
>
> And it's Friday night and it's kicking in
> In that pink dress, they're gonna crucify me
> Oh, and you in all your vibrant youth
> How could anything bad ever happen to you?
> You make a fool of death with your beauty, and
> for a moment
> I forget to worry
> (Florence and the Machine, "Hunger")

Chapter 17

Freedom

Right now I'm in a state of mind,
I wanna be in like all the time

—"No Tears Left to Cry" by Ariana Grande

So the question remains: what do I DO?

I came back to Mission Bay Beach to sit with this question in the waiting period. It's where I most prevalently first saw the pathway of life. So I figure this is the best place to sit and listen for His direction.

Still, I'm not hearing too much. But I'm dancing, and I'm vibing. I know that when the time is right I'll hear what the correct next step is. Following this voice is what led us to this pathway of life essentially, so we can be confident that this voice will speak to us again. And we can be confident that we will be able to identify it once we hear it.

But since I have a lot of time to think, maybe I can continue to improve my brain mechanisms by training my brain to listen for His direction better.

Maybe the question that I am asking isn't the right question.

"What do I do?" This question is still centered around my ego. What do I do? If I've learned anything from this trauma, it's that listening to my ego first has not led me down a positive road.

So maybe I should rephrase the question: how do I make the world a better place?

Again, I guess this question is centered around my ego as well. It's still centered around me. Yes, it has better intention, but still egocentric. Hmmm...

Maybe the question is "What do YOU want me to do?"

This one's a lot harder to grasp. Because in order to answer it, I really need to fully trust you. Like 100%. Completely. Because it would be impossible to completely release that rope around my ankle unless I was POSITIVE that I could swim to the top. I've had that rope around my ankle for so long that if I take it off completely I don't even know if I can swim anymore.

I recognize that this is something I will need to work on every day. I won't 100% fully trust you until I fully enter your pathway at the end of my life on this earth. But I can confidently look at this journey and decide that I'm trusting you 99.9% now and that the rest of my life will be working on that 0.1% that I still have left.

Arash was part of the 0.5% who was diagnosed with anaplastic astrocytoma. Maybe this just meant that he had already reached that 0.1% that he had left to fully trust you.

*****

My mind can't help but wander back to that interview question that I completely bombed the other day.

Now, I've found that when your heart and mind wander, it usually brings you to where your passion lies.

Over the past few weeks, I've gone on multiple job interviews and applied to multiple different kind of nursing jobs, but when I spend time sitting with the pathway of life at Mission Bay, I find my mind going back to that interview.

I also think our mind goes to places where we've made mistakes, made mishaps, or felt extremely uncomfortable when our minds wander.

This used to cause severe anxiety and distress, but now it doesn't because we have let go of that rope around our ankles and we are swimming up to the surface. So now I can confidently say that I look at these mistakes, mishaps, and uncomfortable moments as opportunities to learn and grow. These are good things.

When I reflect on the four job interviews that I've gone on since I arrived here, the one from the surgery center stands out the most to me. And this was the interview where I royally screwed up. The other three job interviews that I went on, I did well. I answered all the questions in a professional manner, and I was offered a job at all 3 of these interviews. However, none of these jobs really lit a fire in me. I never really thought about the pathway when I was at these jobs. I mean, yes, I knew the pathway was there. Because as we know, it always is. But during these interviews, I never had a head-to-head or conflicting moment with the pathway like I did in the surgery center interview. All 3 interviews prior to this one went pretty smoothly. Nothing out of the norm at any of these interviews. I didn't feel particularly challenged by any of the questions, and I didn't leave the interview with any strong feelings either for the job or against the job. They were fine. They were jobs. I'm sure that if I accepted the offers at any of these places, I would grow to like the job and it would all be fine. But I declined the offer for all 3.

Yes, I am aware that I am eating microwave popcorn for meals and I am currently paying for two rents with no job! Ha!

But that voice still lingered…the voice that brought me to California…that I should wait. I shouldn't just accept one of these jobs knowing that this is not the job for me. I shouldn't just go with the safe option and accept one of the first jobs that I get offered.

Yes, I realize how crazy I sound!

*****

As I sit with these thoughts, I am genuinely trying to listen to why that is. Why did I not accept one of those jobs? Logically, I need a job. I moved to a new city. I am paying two rents with no salary. I have a car payment. I have utilities to pay for. I need to pay for gas. I need to pay for groceries. I need a job.

But I don't feel that same anxiety, pressure, or urgency that I felt when I was searching for jobs in the past. And from society's perspective, I am worse off currently than I was back in Chicago. Why is that?

I think it's because I decided to trust him. I think my post-PTSD brain mechanisms are finally starting to stick and become a pattern. I am choosing to trust instead of to fear. I am choosing to listen instead of to lead. I am choosing life over death.

So let's make a choice to officially take that rope off from around our ankles and let it sink to the bottom of the ocean. We are strong. We know how to swim. We are now fully making choices to learn and grow on our way to the top of the ocean. We don't make decisions based on what people think about us anymore because we are living for an audience of one now. That ship at the top of the ocean. That pathway. Him.

Chapter 18

The Lifeguard's Boss

I have been procrastinating on this because the surgery center interview was so cringeworthy I don't like to think about it. But we threw that rope off our ankles, so now I'm making choices to learn and grow. And to learn and grow from that interview, I need to reflect on it. Regardless of how cringeworthy it is!

First, LIFE.

Second, listen & decipher.

Third, TRUST.

Fourth, pick LIFE again.

So I arrive at this interview and meet with both the CEO and the director of nursing at this surgery center.

Naturally, I am nervous for this interview. As you are for any interview. But this interview, I was much more nervous than I was for the previous 3 which I think shows how much I actually wanted this job. In the past, I may have let this intense anxiety sway my decision. Maybe I'll just pick one of the other jobs that doesn't seem as challenging, one of the other jobs that didn't make me as anxious or worried prior to the interview. I'll be safer doing that job.

But nah, we won that war already. We're warriors. We're war heroes. So let's work to become ships.

So I walk into this interview and sit down. We start out by making small talk about how I am from Chicago and just moved to San Diego. The interviewers go on to tell me how they have a lot of people from their department who are from the Midwest. Okay, great! Off to a good start.

"So, what made you want to work in a surgery center as opposed to an operating room as in your previous experience?"

I froze. I forgot the pathway existed for a moment. I only had my ego. That trauma resurfaced. Maybe I had a flashback? To be honest with you, I don't know what happened. I don't know if my PTSD just literally hit me on the face and I forgot where I was for a minute or what job I was interviewing for, or if I literally just transported back to Misericordia for a minute because I answered the question like I was interviewing for a nursing job at an inpatient facility in a hospital, which is the exact opposite of the job that I was interviewing for.

"Ummmm…I am passionate about building strong relationships with my patients, and I feel like there is more opportunity to do that here."

What the fork????????? Literally, I am laughing at myself right now. That makes 0 sense. In the operating room, your patient is under anesthesia. You really only talk to them for about 5 minutes. And at a surgery center, you have even less time communicating with the patient because there is less turnover time between cases.

This answer literally makes no sense. It sounds like I don't even know what job I'm interviewing for.

Again, I am laughing. I'm only able to laugh at this mistake instead of going down a spiral of self-loathing and unforgiveness because of that pathway of life. Because of Him.

Even as I'm writing this, I don't know why I answered the question like that. The best I can come up with is that I literally forgot the pathway which led me to forget where I even was. That's how important the pathway is. It's our foundation. It's the truth. It's literally everything. It's all we have, and it's sincerely all we need.

Reflecting on this question, my ego won the battle, and I went into fight-or-flight mode that made me answer the way I perceived the interviewers wanted me to answer. But now even this is different! Because the way that I perceived they wanted me to answer the question was completely wrong! What I thought they wanted to hear in that moment did not make sense, it was NOT what they wanted to hear. My perspective was morphed.

But.

This is actually a good thing.

This is healing. This is good.

Now, when I am not following his path, things don't work out well for me. When I forgot his path for a moment at the interview and I answered the question wrong, the director of nursing stepped in and said, "Well, not really. This is a surgery center, and we have extremely limited time with the patient because the turnover time is higher, and we do about 10–15 cases in an operating room in a day."

This immediately led me back to the pathway. I think I recognized in that moment, for reasons that I will never know or understand, that I forgot the pathway for a minute, which led me to screw up.

In the past, when I was living without the pathway, I didn't have this strong sense of right and wrong. This would have sent me into a downward spiral of self-loathing, and I don't know if I would have recovered in that interview.

And I think that these new post-PTSD brain mechanisms are finally kicking in. And that now when I forget the pathway and my subconscious/ego kicks in and answers how I perceive people and society wants me to, that answer is actually incorrect. It is untruthful. And not accurate. I will not move forward with this kind of thinking. Instead, I will actually screw up, which forces me back to the correct pathway. So basically, my subconscious is now trained in alignment with the pathway, not with society/what other people think.

I forgot the pathway in this interview, and I subconsciously answered the first question incorrectly, but this time, He threw the life buoy to me to remind me to focus on him first. I wasn't the one who called 911. He threw me that life buoy to get me back on track in the interview.

But his life buoy has a different word on it: *Refocus*. On the pathway. On Him.

First, pathway of LIFE.

Second, listen & decipher.

Third, TRUST.

Fourth, LIFE again.

Okay, next question.

"What sparked your initial interest in the operating room/what is your favorite thing and least favorite thing about the operating room?"

Now that I am refocused, I answered this question truthfully and accurately.

I continued to do this for the rest of the questions.

I was able to breathe after I refocused. That hiccup almost reminded me that it's different this time. You are going to forget about your ego for this interview and answer with me as your most important focus. It does not matter what these people think about you. I mean, essentially, yes, it does. But their opinions aren't as important as mine. He literally threw me a life buoy—REFOCUS—at the beginning of this interview, ultimately allowing me to breathe and then answer the remaining questions accurately and truthfully.

This interview was a current, and I was able to learn and grow from it. Yes, I initially let my ego win, but I followed the plan:

First, pathway of LIFE.

Second, listen & decipher.

Third, TRUST.

Fourth, LIFE.

And I chose LIFE after I messed up. Immediately. That old habit of choosing ego again and again and again has been broken! Yes, it's going to happen. We're human. We're going to make mistakes. It's going to happen, but now our subconscious is trained to bring us back to the path. To Him. So we can take a deep breath. We're going to be fine. It's just a current. We're learning & growing from this.

I continued on with the interview and sincerely enjoyed talking with both ladies. They gave me a quick tour of their operating room at the end of the interview, and I even joked, "I'm so sorry about that first question, I literally don't know what happened."

*****

So I'm sitting here again in the waiting period with that pathway, and I'm waiting on the answer to "What do YOU want me to do?"

I think I'm starting to understand why I did not take those first 3 job interviews. The pathway wasn't really present during them. But during this interview, the pathway was screaming to me. And when I reflect on this, I remember when this same pathway was screaming to me at Northwestern and Misericordia.

I am coming to terms with how different this voice sounded to me then versus now.

When I was at Northwestern, I was still attached to that anchor. My main motivation was still protecting my fragile ego. My decisions were made out of fear. My decisions were made depending on the currents and people's perceptions of me. I was still trying to prevent myself from sinking down into the bottom of the sea. So when this voice screamed to me at Northwestern, this was a voice of concern and safety. At the time, I needed to leave. There was no growth or learning for me during that current because I was still fighting this battle with the anchor. I was still in survival mode. And that voice was protecting me. I was not in a place for learning and growth at that time. & that is okay.

When I walked by the Lakefront after leaving Northwestern, that voice assured me that I made the right decision by directing my focus to the ship out on the lake.

When I left Misericordia because I was having panic attacks, this was the voice screaming to me as well. There is no learning or growth for me here at this time because I was still in survival mode. This voice was protecting me. And I needed this extreme warning sign to ultimately leave and listen to him.

*****

Now, my brain mechanisms have changed. They are the post-PTSD ship over ego-focused brain mechanisms. They are becoming patterns with more and more practice.

Now, when this voice screamed to me in this interview, I had a completely different reaction. I did not walk out the door, I did not have a panic attack. I did not fight this voice or pretend that I knew better. I am fully aware that this voice knows better than I do. I was not afraid of this voice anymore. I recognized that this voice is trying to protect me. I am safe with this voice. I'm glad this voice intervened on my behalf. This is the voice of the lifeguard's boss. It's His voice. & now, I responded to this voice by refocusing my highest priority on Him, and then I continued to proceed in the interview by answering the questions truthfully and to the best of my ability.

*****

I received a call from the recruiting hirer two days later: "San Diego Surgery would like you to meet the charge OR nurse for a second-round interview. I heard you were a little nervous at the first one. Best of luck!"

*****

The interviewers had shown me grace. Thank you, God, for this second chance.

Chapter 19

Forgiving Ourselves

I guess it's pretty safe to say that we should follow wherever the pathway is most prevalent. And typically, I found that the most challenging road is where the pathway is.

But this shouldn't be discouraging. This should actually be inspiring.

We have absolutely everything we need to follow this path.

"So do not fear, for I am with you; do not be dismayed, for I am your God. I will strengthen you and help you; I will uphold you with my righteous right hand" (Isaiah 41:10).

I remember what my dad said to me when Arash was diagnosed with brain cancer: "It's pretty clear what the right thing to do here is."

For so long, I thought I knew what the right thing to do was. But after seeing this pathway, I now *know* what the right thing to do is. Does that mean I'm going to do it every time? Definitely not. Our ego will kick in. Our ego will cause us to make mistakes and missteps. But this shouldn't discourage us or scare us because we know that the pathway is protecting us. It's the lifeguard's boss! It is good. It is beautiful. It will only give us what we can handle. And when we can't handle it and our egos win the battle and we forget the pathway (or forget where we are, such as I did in the interview), the pathway will correct us. It'll protect us.

Inevitably, we will have doubts. I'm making a conscious decision right now that when I doubt this, I am going to remember Arash willingly choosing to get baptized and grasping that rosary on his last day, and I am going to remember him saying goodbye to me across the bay at Mission Beach. The Pathway of Life. It's His voice now.

*****

I think one of the things I struggled most with while Arash was sick was the uncertainty of it all. For so long, you have a road map planned out in your head. "Okay. I'm going to go to school. Now I'm going to get a job. I'm going to meet someone," etc., etc. Whatever plan that is, and this typically works out. Yes, you definitely face some challenges along the way. You may fail a class or not get the job you anticipated or whatever that may be. But the uncertainty with grief is different. This is the uncertainty of eternity. This is looking death in the face and deciding how you can hold on to control for as long as possible before it's taken away from you. The uncertainty with grief is the realization that you're not in control. And your future is completely uncertain. I think this is a very scary concept. To think that you have no control in how your life is going to play out is terrifying. But isn't trauma terrifying? Isn't protecting your ego for the rest of your life more terrifying? Isn't becoming exhausted by grasping on to your ankle terrifying?

Isn't being a prisoner to the anchor for the rest of your life the most terrifying thing of all?

When Arash was diagnosed with cancer and we were told his prognosis was about 7 months, I found foundation, security, and trust in this. Okay, we can plan accordingly. We can make the best of this. We can stretch this out as long as possible. We can make every day count. We have 7 months. I trusted this information. I found comfort in that timeline. It was a sense of truth, a sense of foundation. A sense of time. I didn't have to directly face eternity yet. We had 7 months left.

But you can't rely on this timeline for foundation. You cannot place your trust in this. This cannot be your ship. Essentially, this is an extremely educated guess. After seeing surgery fail, chemotherapy fail, medications fail, physical therapy fail, speech pathology fail, you are forced to look deeper than medicine for foundation and trust.

At the time, this was terrifying. I woke up every day for a year not knowing what was going to happen or when it was going to happen, and this caused so much pain, so much anxiety, so much fear, so much loneliness, so much substance abuse, so much suffering.

Looking back on it, if I had been able to find the beauty in giving up control to this ship earlier, I could have enjoyed more moments with Arash in his last year in this life. I could have saved myself a lot of suffering and agony if I had stopped trying to protect my ego from the fear of uncertainty.

But I understand that again, this is an easy concept to grasp. "If I had known then, what I know now…"

But that's the whole point of trauma. It's meant to completely break you down and build you up. The process is occurring so that you learn to trust Him. If we were born already trusting him 100%, then there wouldn't be a need for that anchor in the first place. That anchor, that pain, that suffering, that trauma is what saved you from getting swept up into the eye of the hurricane in the infinite ocean. Without trauma, you have no foundation. If we can change the way we think about trauma, we can truly change the world.

*****

Another thing I truly struggled with while Arash was sick was learning to forgive myself. For so long, I thought that God was doing this to punish me for all the wrongs I had done in my past. For every person I hurt both intentionally and unintentionally, I truly believed that God hated me for those mistakes and flaws. I thought that this was His way of getting even with me for years of not listening to Him and letting my ego win over and over while hurting anyone that was in my path.

Arash really was the one who taught me to forgive myself. Arash loved me unconditionally. I could be having the absolute worst day in the world with anxiety pouring out of every inch of me, and Arash would be there for me. Every single time. While I was working through the COVID pandemic and I was facing the uncertainty of that, Arash was with me every single night to wipe my tears or listen to me vent. He built me up during those times. He called me when I was anxious. He encouraged me to keep going despite all odds. He forgave me for absolutely every mistake, every mean thing I said, every overreaction, everything. He helped me to believe in myself and love myself. I'm forever grateful for that.

Arash taught me how to love first. He loved me perfectly. And because he did this, I was able to be with him through this journey. Yes, I was in pain, I was suffering. But I can honestly say that I never once thought of actually leaving him. And he never tried to leave me after this diagnosis. That was divine intervention.

There is simply no other way. I didn't have the strength to get through that year of pain and the months that followed without a higher power. I can't imagine how Arash alone had the strength to endure that debilitating disease. The strength was in the pathway. It was in Him. Arash had seen it first. He saw the path before I even met him. It's why he was so different. It's why he was so unique. It's why he loved me unconditionally and he loved others unconditionally. It's why he was so confident and secure. It's why he had so much joy and loved to travel. It's why he could never sit still. It's why he could see the beauty and wonder of the world that I couldn't quite fully see or understand yet. He had seen the path. He was in the last 0.1% of learning to fully trust Him.

Again, I will never understand why this would happen to a family. I will never understand why a twenty-six-year-old was diagnosed with terminal brain cancer.

But if the last year of suffering was Arash's final 0.1% test of his complete trust in Him to finally see that beautiful pathway to an eternity of beauty and wonder that I was blessed to have witnessed with him for the 3 years prior to his diagnosis, then I wouldn't give up that 0.1% of pain and suffering for anything in the world.

*****

One of the first things I did when I arrived in San Diego was to go to Sunset Cliffs. I have been there twice previously. The first time was with Arash and our friends Mitch and Maris. The second time was with my sister, Shannon, in June of last year. I love Sunset Cliffs, it's honestly one of the reasons I moved to San Diego. When you're sitting on those cliffs overlooking the Pacific Ocean and watching the perfect sun setting over the infinite ocean, you feel that divine intervention. The only other place I've felt this divine intervention to this magnitude was at the Cliffs of Moher in Ireland, when I went with Arash in 2019. It is stunning. It is inspiring. That feeling of no anxiety, no agitation; only peace is prevalent at Sunset Cliffs. You feel the warmth of the sunset in your heart, you can feel the ease of the waves in your bloodstream. When you come to Sunset Cliffs, you feel like you've been there before. Similar to how I felt when I met Arash. When you come to Sunset Cliffs, you feel like you're catching up with an old friend. When you come to Sunset Cliffs, it feels like you've just stepped off the plane in Ireland and the cliffs are welcoming you home. You are certain of the pathway here. You are certain of the good infinity awaiting you. And when the sun sets, it inspires you to look forward to tomorrow's.

I went to Sunset Cliffs with a friend who is from San Diego. He showed me a part of the cliffs that I had never seen before. You can actually scale part of the cliffs using a rope that's secured to the cliffs to get down to the shore to watch the sunset by the rocky shore.

At first, I was extremely hesitant to use this rope to climb down the hills. They are steep, and I wasn't wearing the right shoes! Ha!

But ultimately.

First, LIFE.

Second, listen & decipher,

Third, TRUST.

Fourth, LIFE again.

I chose to climb down using the rope.

We watched the sunset sitting right off the shore, and I've never seen something so beautiful before. The red, pink, and orange sky lands perfectly over the infinite edge of the water.

The sun setting perfectly over the ocean is the pathway. The perfection of this moment has to be divine intervention. There is no way that this could have been created by anything other than God. The beauty speaks for itself.

*****

During the COVID-19 pandemic, in the summer of 2020, I had a health scare. Something concerning showed up on my annual pap smear, and I had to have a biopsy done. Fortunately, the sample was benign, and that was really the end of it. But reflecting on this, Arash first demonstrated perfect love to me then.

I've buried this memory and this fear so deep into my subconscious I'm really just remembering this now as I'm writing this. I've always associated this memory with fear, anxiety, worry. It was an anchor. An anchor that was so painful I forgot about it until just now.

When my gynecologist told me that they found something abnormal on my pap smear and I needed to come in for a biopsy, my world came to a screeching halt. Looking back on this, it's because I had no foundation. I had no anchor; I had no ship. And when you hear bad news when you don't have this pathway to follow, you have no choice but to completely lose control and spiral into fear, doubt, worry, anxiety. This type of news will send you into a hurricane in the sea if you have no anchor to ground you or you have no ship to follow for guidance.

And that's exactly what happened. I lost it. The fear and anxiety completely overwhelmed me. I hadn't seen the pathway yet. I had no foundation. I was swimming in a terrible hurricane. I let the flooding of California sweep me into the hurricane. I let the flooding of California prohibit me from making the trip. I let the flooding of California prevent me from hearing His voice and following it. The flooding of California swept me into a hurricane in the ocean, and I had no lifeguard to call. I had no life buoy to grab on to. All I had were the fears, doubts, worry, anxiety of the harshest current I had ever seen at that point. All I had was my precious little ego that doesn't stand a chance in a hurricane in the ocean.

So again, I am thankful for this anchor that we have conquered. That He has conquered. Because without that anchor, you wouldn't escape the hurricane of the ocean. You would still be in this horrific storm. You wouldn't have been given the opportunity to finally see the ship, the higher power, the pathway of life, His voice.

So, yes, the anchor is trauma. It took pain and suffering to get it. But for that, we are thankful. It allowed us to see the ship. There is no point in looking at this trauma and still feeling imprisoned by it. There is no point in still looking at this anchor and continuing to not forgive yourself for the mistakes, missteps, and wrongs that it took to get here.

Actually, at this point, knowing what we know: the truth of the ship. The truth of the pathway of life. The truth of Him. To still beat yourself up for the pain and suffering, to still not forgive yourself for the mistakes and missteps that it took you to get to this point would actually be deliberately not listening to the ship. To still feel like you are not worthy of the ship or loved by the ship would actually be choosing your ego over his voice.

And we have established from this point on. We are listening to the pathway of life. We are working every day to choose that ship over our ego.

It's the only way to go forward.

So forgive yourself. He did.

*****

Sorry, I digress!

Back to my health scare. I was terrified because I had no foundation.

At the time, I was terrified to tell Arash about this scare. We had a plan! We were going to get married and have kids. If I tell Arash, he's going to be so upset. If I tell Arash, he might change his mind about me. And what if this actually is cancer, and what if I actually cannot have kids? Would he leave me? Would he not love me?

Again, I was making all these assumptions before I had even gotten the results of the biopsy. I'm seeing now that this is what happens when you have no foundation. Your ego takes control. You have no other option. I had no idea what the results of this test were yet. But I was in the hurricane, and at that point, my destination was the eye of the storm.

So I assumed the worst-possible outcome because I hadn't had the anchor yet that was attaching me to the ship. All I knew is that they saw something abnormal and wanted to do a biopsy to be safe. But I took control of the situation and assumed the worst because I had no ship. I assumed that I had cancer or couldn't have kids. That was my ego. That was fear. I was in the hurricane.

But reflecting, I let my ego win because I didn't have any other option. I was in the hurricane of the ocean. I had no foundation.

I went back and forth with this information. Do I tell Arash or not?

We were living together and quarantining together at the time, and this fear was eating me alive. Arash and I told each other everything, so it was very difficult to try to keep this from him.

My mind was spiraling in that hurricane, and I ultimately told him about the abnormal result and how I was afraid I might have cancer or not be able to have kids.

Arash gave me a hug and told me the same thing my mom told me on Friday the 13th when he was diagnosed with brain cancer: "It's going to be okay."

Wow.

My anxieties, my fears, my worries disappeared in that moment. I was truly overwhelmed by how completely selfless this love was. I basically had just told Arash that I didn't know if our future was going to be what we had planned, and instead of running away or questioning me or our relationship, he embraced it. And comforted me at my lowest moment.

Reflecting on this, Arash demonstrated this type of love because he had seen the pathway already. He wasn't afraid of eternity. He had an anchor already from his previous brain tumor, and he was on his way to becoming a ship. He chose to be there for me. He chose to stay with me regardless of the outcome of that biopsy because he wasn't afraid of the journey ahead. He already knew about the ship. He knew this ship could weather all storms and this health scare was just a storm in the ocean. He knew it would pass. He wasn't afraid.

Reflecting on when Arash was sick, this is probably the reason why he was able to stay so positive throughout the entire diagnosis. Like I mentioned previously, he never complained. He was never angry. Never bitter.

I can say with complete honesty that I never heard him once say "This isn't fair" or "Why me?" There's no other explanation as to why he could be this positive. He had seen the ship. He knew he was on his way to it.

If Arash hadn't seen the pathway or the ship during his diagnosis, then he would have been like me when I had my health scare: lost in the hurricane of fear, worry, and uncertainty with neither an anchor nor a ship to grab on to.

God gives you what you can handle.

*****

Reflecting again on my health scare that is just now resurfacing in my brain, I think one of the things I struggled with the most at that time was that similar to when Arash was first diagnosed with brain cancer, I truly thought that God was punishing me. I truly believed that God was angry at me for all the wrong I had done in the past and this was his way of saying, "Oh, all those plans you want for your future? No way. You don't deserve that. Look at all the horrible mistakes you've made in your life."

Like I said, I was in the hurricane and the flooding in California was the center of the storm. I had no truth, no foundation.

For many nights, I would lay awake, beating myself up for all the mistakes I made. I was in an endless spiral of self-loathing, and I was unable to forgive myself.

This may be the hardest part of surviving and escaping the hurricane: forgiving yourself.

Just as much as your ego can sway you to be too prideful and too confident that you believe you don't need the ship, so can your ego sway you to be too critical and too harsh that you don't believe you're worthy of the ship. It's really a double-edged sword in the internal battle that we're battling every day.

Arash's love for me in that moment is the closest thing to perfect love that I've ever experienced. I came to Arash with all my flaws, my imperfections, my fears, my past mistakes, my insecurities, my doubts. Everything. And he told me it was going to be okay. He still loved me. He wasn't going anywhere.

That pathway demonstrated this love to Arash previously; it's how he was able to get out of the hurricane. It's what gave him the anchor and the ship. It's what allowed him to show me this kind of love when I was still stuck in the storm.

*****

Now, that we're looking at anchors differently, I'm going to look at this anchor that resurfaced differently. I'm going to sit with it and really think about it. (Again, I am still under the illusion I can afford to live in San Diego without a job.)

Note: I'm noticing that after being diagnosed with PTSD, I'm becoming more conscious of my memories and flashbacks. When I was attached to the anchor, these flashbacks would cause extreme distress, anxiety, and ultimately panic attacks.

I also think that memories and anchors resurfacing during situations that trigger them isn't specific to PTSD. I think it's also universal. Of course, you're going to remember troubling times in your life from time to time. And these memories will occur in situations that trigger the resurfacing of that anxiety and fear. Those memories and flashbacks are part of you. They brought you to the anchor. So let's change the way we look at them so they no longer cause us extreme distress, anxiety, or panic.

First, life.

Second, listen.

Third, trust.

Fourth, life again.

I think that part of the reason these flashbacks of Arash being sick caused so much anxiety was because I still had not fully seen the pathway of life yet. I was still associating these flashbacks of Arash's seizures and physical and mental decline with his death. When these flashbacks or memories would resurface, my mind was still picking death first. My mind was still going to his funeral and his casket. It was still picking the anchor.

After generations and generations of trauma, this was a learned brain mechanism. We know that the anchor is turning to a ship now. We know that because Arash was baptized and on his last day, he was grasping on to that rosary with Jesus on a cross with all the strength that he had left. He could not walk. He could not talk. He couldn't speak. But he was holding on to that rosary with all his strength. He was about to enter the pathway. His pathway.

That happened. That was real.

So we have to make a conscious decision now to pick the pathway of life over death.

I think this is so difficult because we still don't fully believe that we are forgiven. We still don't believe that we are worthy of this unconditional love.

For example, when I had a health scare and thought my biopsy was going to be cancerous, my subconscious picked death over life. It automatically assumed that I had cancer and was going to die. But this was a learned brain mechanism from generations and generations of trauma. So you need to forgive yourself. Remember, you are but a drop in the infinity of the ocean. To hold yourself to the standards of this ocean and this perfect ship up above would be completely unrealistic and quite frankly impossible.

Our egos are nothing compared to the greatness of this ship. So let's humble ourselves and be happy about this. This is freedom. This is finally taking the chain off the anchor. We need to forgive ourselves for our lives prior. We cannot hold ourselves to impossible standards. Just like self-loathing is pointless, so is holding ourselves to the impossible standards of the infinite ocean and the ship.

Arash saw the pathway first, and he forgave me perfectly because he already knew he was forgiven.

"Humble yourselves, then, under God's mighty hand, so that he will lift you up in his own good time. Leave all your worries with Him, because he cares for you" (1 Peter 5:6–7).

*****

So now, when a memory resurfaces of Arash being sick or even when a memory resurfaces of any other type of trauma or challenge we have faced in the past resurfaces, we know we can pick life first. So we can make a conscious decision to pick the pathway of life first. I'm making a conscious choice to now associate all my flashbacks and memories with Mission Beach Bay and the pathway of life.

The more I practice making this conscious decision, the more I will train my subconscious so inevitably when my ego wins the battle my subconscious will remind it to refocus on the pathway of life (a.k.a. the lifeguard's boss will take over).

So to pick death first would be pointless and a waste of time. He forgave us so we can forgive ourselves.

Let's not waste our time, there's too much beauty and wonder in this world! We're on our way to seeing it!

*****

In a way, we're turning all our demons from PTSD to angels of new life.

Chapter 20

Forgiving Others

Now that we have established that not forgiving ourselves would be pointless and a waste of time, we can now fully forgive ourselves and extend that forgiveness to others.

When I reflect on my time at Northwestern and how overly sensitive I was to the criticism and feedback I was receiving, I am recognizing that I had not fully forgiven myself at that point, so it was impossible for me to forgive others yet. My thinking was still completely egocentric and was still in survival mode, trying not to let that anchor completely engulf me. And I'm realizing that is okay.

Grief is real. It's a process. We shouldn't be so hard on ourselves. We should be kinder to ourselves. We should allow ourselves to take the time to heal. And we shouldn't feel so guilty about it. That journey to the bottom of the ocean is essential.

Now that I fully realize that I am forgiven and I am excited about living for this pathway of life now, I am going to make a conscious choice to forgive other people in all situations and circumstances.

"For if you forgive other people when they sin against you, your Heavenly Father will also forgive you" (Matthew 6:14–15).

*****

I think forgiving ourselves is the hardest part of the entire process. Because in order to forgive yourself, you have to truly 100% trust. You have to completely trust that the ship you are now dedicating your life to following is good. You have to completely trust that this ship is not angry or punishing.

For so much of my life, I truly thought the ship was punishing me for mistakes I had made. I truly thought I wasn't worthy of forgiveness. Again, I think this is a result of generations and generations of trauma. Just as the ship's beauty and wonder is incomprehensible to our minds, the magnitude of this trauma and grief of the anchor is also incomprehensible. So to try to analyze and justify every mistake you've made in the past is also pointless and a waste of time.

I did that for years, and all that did was cause pain, suffering, and anxiety.

But now that I have watched my love, Arash, willingly get baptized while he was essentially on his deathbed, I have no doubt in my mind that this pathway is real. There is a good ship. The pain and suffering that we go through in this life is not for no reason. It's not a punishment for our egotistical ways and past mistakes. This pain and suffering is transformative. This is how you escape the hurricane. This is how you get your foundation grounded in that anchor. This is the lifeguard's boss tossing you that life buoy. It's what leads you to the ship, the Pathway of Life.

If you're going through a stormy season in life, stay strong. He's picked you because he knows you are strong and can handle what is ahead of you. He will only give you what you can handle. Keep your eye on the ship.

*****

I'm finding that the more forgiving I am with myself, the more forgiving with others I am. Again, we're all just fish swimming in this crazy ocean! We have to help each other swim to the top!

As I've mentioned for most of my life, I've been overly sensitive to everyone's opinion of me. I thought if I acted a certain way, then I could make people like me. I could control the opinions of others by my actions and my words. As I type that, I am realizing how absolutely insane that is. How in the world would I be able to control what another person thinks of me? I couldn't even control the rope that was around my ankle. How in the world would I have the power to actually direct or sway the current of the ocean? It's simple: I don't. So just another thing I can cross off my list of worries now that I am following the ship. This is a complete waste of time. It is pointless. I'm a drop in the ocean. I don't have the power to control the perspectives, opinions, and thoughts of other people.

This used to cause me so much distress.

I find my thoughts always steering me back to the operating room. I think this is that voice subtly nudging me there. I've been waiting for that nudge for a while. The operating room has been the most challenging place for me but also has been the place I'm finding that I have the most opportunities to grow. Maybe that's the direction of the path? Maybe if we identify where our strengths and weaknesses are, we can seek to go to places where there is the most opportunity for growth. For us and for others. I mean, after all, we know this path isn't going to be easy. But we're up for the challenge, we're badass ships now.

*****

I digress, again! I think that's the path's way of recognizing my ego and tossing me a life buoy. *Refocus.*

*****

The operating room can be an extremely stressful place, as you can imagine. There is every type of personality that you can imagine here. Most of the time, surgeries go exactly as planned. However, when things don't go exactly as planned, the tension rises quickly, and the mix of personalities can get extremely colorful. To put it politely. When things don't go as planned during surgery, you have to act immediately. That means all bedside manner or even just basic human social interaction skills can get completely tossed out the window. And as a result, there can be a lot of yelling and tense moments.

When I worked at Elmhurst and I was still attached to the anchor, I would take these tense moments to heart. I would sincerely think less of myself if a surgeon yelled at me or made a snide remark at me during a surgery. I would obsess over the criticism. "What did I do wrong?" And I would fall into that cycle of self-loathing and inability to forgive myself. I'm realizing that was because I hadn't fully found my foundation yet. So I was swayed by the current of that particular surgical case. Which I now realize is insane!

I'm going to take the time and break this down again. (Again, how much longer can I live on microwave popcorn for?)

First, life.

Second, listen.

Third, trust.

Fourth, life.

One situation in the operating room always sticks out for me. It was a routine spinal fusion procedure that suddenly turned emergent in the middle of the surgery. The patient needed a cardiovascular surgeon and blood immediately. I was the circulating nurse at this time, and it was my job to page the cardiovascular surgeon and order/retrieve the blood for the patient. The stakes were high. The tensions were higher, and everyone in the operating room was in crisis mode. This was a huge deal!

The surgeon screamed at me, "Megan! What's taking so long?! Do you even know what you're doing!?"

I immediately questioned myself. I had already paged for the cardiovascular surgeon, notified the operating room director, and ordered the blood STAT. It just had not arrived yet. Essentially, I did absolutely everything I had control over that needed to be done in this moment of crisis.

But this still caused me extreme distress and anxiety. My immediate reaction was to double-guess everything I was doing and conclude that the surgeon was on to something, I don't know what I'm doing. He was right. I'm a horrible nurse. This wouldn't have even happened if I knew what I was doing.

Note: This surgeon was a good friend of mine and is an extremely skilled and intelligent surgeon. This was an extremely challenging case, and the patient survived and recovered perfectly healthy.

*****

Now that we're not thinking of currents in terms of peoples' perspectives, opinions, and critiques of us anymore, we can actively search for currents that align with our strengths and values and can help us grow where we are weak. We can actively seek out opportunities where we can use our strengths to help others. We can actively seek out opportunities for growth so we can become ships.

A surgical case is a great example of a current. I guess we can try to define currents more specifically now as we are actively seeking currents that will help us utilize our strengths to grow and help others.

A surgical case essentially follows the same pattern every time. I'm going to try to look at this on a broad spectrum: the beginning, the middle, and the end. The opening act, the main performance, and closing act.

First, the patient is brought into the operating room, and anesthesia puts the patient to sleep and intubates them, puts a breathing tube into their lungs for surgery.

The main performance: the patient undergoes the surgery they need.

Third, anesthesia extubates them and removes that breathing tube from the patient's lungs, and they wake up from surgery.

So I'm going to look for that higher power's voice on guidance to how I can use my strengths to help in this current and ways that my weaknesses can grow in this current.

First, as a circulating nurse, it is my job to stand and assist anesthesia with intubating as needed; 9.9/10 times, there are no problems intubating the patient, but every once in a while, anesthesia will need me to call for backup and/or additional equipment that may be needed to assist with intubation.

When I was a new nurse in the operating room, this, of course, caused me anxiety and stress. I was in the hurricane, and I would always assume the worst possible outcome at first. What if the intubation doesn't go as planned? What if there's an emergency and anesthesia needs help and I don't know how to help them!

First, life.

Second, listen.

Third, trust.

Fourth, pick. Life again.

Looking at this specific example. One time when I was a circulating nurse at Elmhurst, anesthesia was having trouble finding the patient's trachea using just a laryngoscope, so they needed a GlideScope, which is a more invasive camera that allows anesthesia to view the patient's trachea better. At Elmhurst, we only had a few of these in the entire unit, and they were in the anesthesia tech storage room. So the anesthesiologist asked me to run and grab the glide scope.

I vividly remember this fear that I had. I think to myself, *I need to sprint to get this, otherwise anesthesia won't be able to intubate and something horrible is going to happen.*

So I sprinted to get the GlideScope and returned, and anesthesia was able to intubate the patient completely safely and effectively.

Phew, I think.

Reflecting on this, I experienced so much fear and anxiety when the intubation didn't go as planned because I was still picking death first. When things didn't go as planned, I immediately assumed the worst. I was in the hurricane with the center of the storm as my destination. My immediate reaction was to sprint to get the GlideScope, and I was terrified that the intubation was going to be a failure and something horrible would happen.

If I break this down, yes, I reacted. Yes, I did what I needed to do. This is a surgery, the patient is under anesthesia, it is a big deal when things don't go as planned, and yes, I needed to sprint to get the GlideScope. Everything I did in that situation was correct.

But do I need to feel this extreme level of stress and anxiety when things don't go as planned anymore? Essentially, how can I change my brain mechanisms so that I am again able to perform at the high necessary level in surgery without letting this anxiety and stress overwhelm me to a point that it is inhibiting me from functioning at the highest level possible for the patient?

Now that I have forgiven myself and I have forgiven others at Northwestern, I really need to look at the root cause of why I wasn't able to perform at the same level at the Northwestern Operating Room as I was in the Elmhurst Operating Room. Yes, I recognize that Northwestern is the best hospital in Illinois. But as we've seen, no hospital is perfect. Northwestern wasn't able to help Arash. No hospital is able to save every patient, so it really doesn't matter what the ranking of the hospital is. I mean, yes, it does. But in what we're focusing on with changing our brain mechanisms post-PTSD, it doesn't. Every hospital is the same.

I'm realizing that when you're trying to heal from trauma or grief, it really doesn't matter what your surroundings are or what your environment is. For so long, I thought I wasn't able to recover because of the environment I was in. I left Elmhurst because I thought that was the cause of my anxiety, I left Northwestern because I thought that was the cause of my anxiety. Same with Misericordia. And ultimately, Chicago.

But after driving thirty hours to California and really sitting with my thoughts and with the pathway and hearing His voice as clearly as I ever have, I'm realizing that it was never my environment that was the problem. It was my battle with the higher power that was the problem. It was my inability to give up control to that higher power. His pathway. The pathway of life.

And now that we know the pathway is with us absolutely everywhere we go, we can conclude that our environment isn't the actual problem we are facing. Yes, it can be good to change environments for our mental and physical health. Yes, it's good to frequent environments where we see the pathway more prevalently and should seek opportunities to sit with this pathway in peace.

But it isn't the root cause of the problem we are facing. Any environment or current is going to have stressors. Any environment or current, you are going to face the perspectives, opinions, and critiques of others. Yes, these stressors can vary in severity from environment to environment. And when changing currents or environments, it's essential to sit in that waiting period and keep dancing and listen to His voice for how to proceed.

But we know the truth now. Of the pathway of life. We know the truth of the ship. And because we know this, we can look at the currents of the ocean and realize that our ego is unable to direct these currents. Yes, we can swim to different ones. But sometimes the current is too strong and we can't swim to another current. We have to adapt to the current we are in.

Another thing that I love and hate about the OR is that every decision is basically ego versus higher power. Every situation needs to be made on the spot. There's no time to sit and dance in the waiting period. There is a patient under anesthesia! You need to shut that ego down quick and react for the patient that is under anesthesia. And I'm learning to embrace that. This is good. This is a good challenge. You know that you're not alone, you have team members surrounding you, just like fish in the ocean. And we are now helping each other to keep dancing toward that ship. So let's not be afraid to lean on people when we need it and to be that person who isn't afraid to go where there is pain, sorrow, worry, or fear. We are strong. We are ships. We can swim to those harsh currents and help other fish get through these currents. This is great. This is freedom. This is really living!

*****

I digress, again. Don't let that ego get too big though. I'm taking that life buoy now. Refocus!

*****

So going back to this example of the intubation, my ego may go into survival mode. This potentially could be a life-or-death situation. So yes, it's human nature to go for your ego first. It's human nature to pick the pathway of death first. And let's not even waste time beating ourselves up about that. At this point, that is absolutely amateur behavior. Do not beat yourself up about this. Forgive yourself quickly, Remember the cross in Arash's hand. Remember the pathway of life. Remember his voice. Remember that the ship is good. The ship is the lifeguard's boss. The ship will throw you that lifebuoy when you need it. Do not fear.

"Fear not, for I am with you. Do not be dismayed. For I am your God. I will strengthen you. Yes, I will help you. Yes, I will uphold you with the right hand of My righteousness" (Isaiah 41:10).

*****

So yes, my ego picks death first. This is where it becomes clear to me that sometimes in life we are not going to be able to leave a current that is causing us distress and fear. Sometimes, the current is too harsh for our egos to be able to swim to another one.

That's why we need to embrace our environment when it's not in our control to swim to another current.

This is a great example of this.

The patient is under anesthesia. I cannot go anywhere. I cannot simply leave the surgery. There is someone under anesthesia! So quick, pathway!

First, life.

Second, listen.

Third, trust.

Fourth, life again.

*****

We're not living for ourselves anymore. We're living for this patient under anesthesia. We are living to better the current we are in. We are learning to grow. We are dancing and vibing with each other to the top. We are part of the operating room team. It's not about us. It's about the team.

That anxiety and fear is now inspiration and motivation.

> Do not be anxious about anything, but in every situation, by prayer and petition, with thanksgiving, present your requests to God. And the peace of God, which transcends all understanding, will guard your hearts and your minds in Christ Jesus. (Philippians 4:6–7)

We are picking life immediately. And we are running to get a GlideScope for the patient. We are strong. We are ships. We got this. He had Arash. He's got us. So we got this.

*****

Tomorrow I have the second-round interview for the surgical center that so graciously gave me a second chance after me completely bombing the first question of the interview.

I'm realizing now that you cannot expect anything in this life to go perfectly. To expect that interview to have gone perfectly with no hiccups was amateur thinking. There's always going to be a mistake or mishap in a current. We can embrace this now and grow from it. No more time for self-loathing. Life's too short. Life's too beautiful. We are ships. And we are actively living to swim with others to the top.

*****

We're alright (oh)
We're always alright (oh)
We're alright (oh)
We're always alright (oh)
We're alright (oh)
We're always alright, alright, we'll be alright (oh)
(Alabama Shakes, "Always Alright")

*****

Chicago Marathon: Mile 24.

Shannon and I are completely exhausted, but a surge of life reignites us. 2 more miles to go, & we have run a marathon. We're running with our hearts. The battery on my phone just ran out, and we don't have any more music. But actually, we have the music of the ship. We're running to that music now.

*****

Okay, great! The intubation of the patient was successful. They are breathing safely. Their vital signs are stable. They are sleeping soundly. They are about to undergo surgery, and they will wake up from anesthesia to begin their journey of recovery & healing.

*****

Okay, so now is the main act. The surgery. The main act.

I'm going to reflect on the previous incident I began explaining earlier where a routine spinal fusion became life-threatening and we needed to page the cardiovascular surgeon immediately and retrieve blood for the patient.

"Megan! What's taking so long?! Do you even know what you're doing?"

First, life.

Second, listen.

Third, trust.

Fourth, life again.

So naturally, my human nature is to pick death first. This is an internal battle that we face every day. So we will continue to struggle with this, but that's okay. The more we practice recognizing that we picked death first and make a conscious decision to pick life, the more we will train our subconscious to pick life so that when our ego wins we can recognize that the lifeguard's boss, Him, is throwing us the life buoy *Refocus* and we pick life. Pick Him. Always.

Okay. So previously when my first reaction was to doubt myself, that was my ego talking. It was picking death.

Now, when this happens in the future, I will pick life. I will recognize that His pathway is sitting right over there. Always. It's not going anywhere. Nothing that anyone says to me, nothing anyone thinks about me can change that. Absolutely nothing can change that.

"And lo, I am with you always, even unto the end of the world" (Matthew 28:20).

So quickly, now that we're living for the patient under anesthesia, we quickly pick life. We are in a current. This is a particularly harsh current. This is life or death. Again, ego versus Him. Pick Him. & know that even when you don't pick Him, he'll throw you that life buoy regardless. Because His love is unconditional. He wants to protect us. He wants to guide us.

We know this. Remember the cross in Arash's hand. Remember the pathway. He could not walk, He could not speak, He could not talk. But he still held on to this cross with his entire strength. That happened. That was real.

So now that we know this, I will quickly brush off this comment from the surgeon. I will recognize that this is a result of the harsh current we are in. He is in the middle of an extremely harsh current. So I'll forgive him quickly. Arash forgave me. He forgave me. The patient is under anesthesia! We don't have time for any of that old nonsense!

Next, I reacted. I did what I needed to do. I paged the cardiovascular surgeon ASAP. I notified the director of the operating room, and he is now in the room. I ordered the blood needed for the patient. The only thing that we are waiting on is for the blood bank to send the blood up to us.

Breathe. Breathe. Breathe.

Remember the pathway. Remember the ship. Remember Him.

This is a current. It'll pass soon. Hang in there.

That life buoy is there for you.

The pathway's not going anywhere.

Now I'm going to recognize that this is a war against boredom at this point. Now, I realize that sounds insane because we have a life-threatening situation going on in the operating room right now. But this really is a war against boredom at this point.

There is nothing else we can do at this moment except wait for the cardiovascular surgeon to arrive to the operating room and for the blood bank to send the blood up.

So we're dancing now. Again, this dancing is a little more tense. Think of it as break dancing. This dancing is tempestuous, turbulent, or energetically unpredictable. We are still vibing, we are still on our way to the ship. But recognize that this is a harsh current. This is a war. Do everything in your power to speed this up. Essentially the current is trying to pull you into that old hurricane, with the eye of the storm as your destination. But keep your eye on the pathway. It's still there. It's not going anywhere. Remember the cross. Remember Arash. Remember Him.

Breathe. Breathe. Breathe.

Pray. Pray. Pray.

"The Lord is my strength and my shield; my heart trusts in him, and he helps me" (Psalm 28:7).

*****

Okay! Phew! The cardiovascular surgeon arrived to the operating room, and the blood bank sent the blood up. The patient is on the way to recovery! Things are stable.

Thank you, Ship!

"In everything give thanks; for this is God's will for you in Christ Jesus" (1 Thessalonians 5:18).

*****

Okay, the surgery is over. Time for the patient to wake up from anesthesia.

This is a little bit harder to think of an example where there was a major challenge during this closing act. Personally, I've never seen a patient not wake up from anesthesia. If there were difficulties during extubation, or if the patient wasn't fully ready to have that breathing tube removed yet, then the patient would be transferred to the post-surgery recovery unit, where they could recover, and when the time was right, they would safely have that tube removed.

Still.

First, life.

Second, listen.

Third, trust.

Fourth, life.

The only thing that really sticks out in my mind is that sometimes when patients wake up from anesthesia, they can be extremely aggressive. Oftentimes, I would need to stand close to anesthesia for assistance during this time while patients are waking up and subconsciously trying to pull that breathing tube out themselves. Patients wake up extremely confused, lethargic, sometimes aggressive and sometimes loopy. It can be very unpredictable.

I'm starting to wonder why I never really witnessed any huge major challenges during this closing act in surgery. Yes, sometimes younger male patients would wake up extremely aggressively. But the OR team would jump in all hands on deck to try to calm the patient down and remind them that they're safe.

I guess maybe it's safe to conclude that patients want to wake up! Subconsciously, we want to wake up & live! We want to enjoy the beautiful journey of life and become ships. There is so much beauty and wonder in this world despite all the challenges and mishaps.

Arash knew this. Arash was dealt an extremely challenging hand of cards. But that didn't stop him from playing the game.

*****

As my mind wanders, I'm also questioning why we completely trust anesthesia. Like, what is it? Propofol is the medication given to patients before and during surgery to cause relaxation and sleepiness. But how do we just know that it's going to work? Every time? It will put a patient to sleep in surgery. Every time. Without fail.

I am working to fully trust His voice the way I trust the propofol that anesthesia gives.

*****

I'm back at Coronado Beach. The place I first came to with Arash back in 2020. And I'm here again. By myself. The ship is still out here. Way across the ocean. The currents and waves of the ocean are coming directly at me. But the ship is standing perfectly still on the edge of the ocean. Perfect white clouds are surrounding this ship.

I'm imagining when I first came here with Arash. Arash was always adamant about actually going into the ocean anytime we went to one. I typically would decline. I'd prefer to sit on the beach and watch the waves roll in the ocean.

I'm realizing now that Arash wasn't afraid of the currents. He never was. He had seen that ship, so he was able to enjoy the currents. He would willingly dive into these currents. Arash willingly welcomed the challenges of life. He thrived on them. He learned from them. He grew from them. I want to get to this point. I want to run into the ocean and dive headfirst into the waves without a care of what the current may bring or without a care at how strong the wave is.

I want to have the trust in the ship that he had.

*****

Hey, hey, haha (where'd you go? Where'd you)
(But now we've found it)
Oh yeah, uh (where'd you go? Where'd you go?
    Where'd you go?)
(Our love was lost, oh, lost)
Doin' the happy dance (where'd you, where'd you
    go?)
(And hope was gone)
Doin' the happy dance (where'd you go? Haha)
Doin' the happy dance (haha, yeah)
Where'd you go? What'd you do?
How the hell you make me fall in love with you?
    (But now we've found it)
And then you leave, now you're gone
All I got is this damn song (and if you flash your
    heart)
So I can feel but I can't touch (oh, heart)
You said my love was a bit too much (I won't
    deny it)
Broke my heart, can't find no crutch
So why don't you come on back home? (Can I
    spit?)
(Mac Miller and the Temper Trap, "Love Lost")

Sometimes, I truly cannot believe this happened. All of it. The beauty of falling in love with Arash and experiencing the beauty and wonder of the world accompanied by the excruciating pain of losing him and the trauma that followed it. I truly sit at night sometimes and I am in complete utter disbelief that this actually happened. It's in moments like these that I have no choice but to look at the pathway and be humbled by this. The magnitude of that greater power is incomprehensible.

I have tried to figure it out for a long time. My mind has been in ultra-drive trying to understand the incomprehensible. But I have completely exhausted my ego. I have no choice but to let go of that rope. I physically can't hold on to it anymore. I don't have the ability to understand this. And I won't understand it until I enter that peaceful pathway. And that's okay. It's the mystery of life that makes it so beautiful. Perfect love doesn't exist without perfect pain. Both are beautiful in their own way. I am a drop in the infinity of the ocean. Arash and I's story was a drop in the ocean. I will love again. He will love again.

I find peace in knowing that he has entered the pathway and that he is safe. He's not suffering anymore. I'm acknowledging that he finally found the ship. He found that beautiful eternity. He was perfectly loved, and it was time for him to go.

God loved him more than I did.

I'm also realizing that it would be a horrible tragedy if I leave what I learned on this journey in that casket.

And before I saw this pathway of Life, I was on the downward spiral of doing just that.

When Arash died, it forced me to ultimately choose life.

When Arash lost his vision, it forced me to see the pathway.

When Arash lost his hearing, it forced me to listen.

When Arash couldn't communicate, it forced me to decipher what that truth was.

When Arash was baptized, it inspired me to believe.

*****

When Arash was healthy, he was always dancing. Now, I understand why.

*****

Whatever you're going through, however deep your trauma is, please keep your hope alive. You wouldn't have gotten this far if He didn't believe you were a warrior or that you were worth the unconditional love of the life buoy. If you're in the hurricane right now with the eye of the storm as your destination, hold on. Hang in there. Do not give up. I know the world can be a dark, dark place. And some nights, it's damn near impossible to see the light at the end of the tunnel. I know that sometimes you can't even find a match to light a candle in that depth of darkness. I know it's nearly impossible to kick that trauma to the bottom of the ocean. And those demons you're facing are uncontrollable. They follow you at every turn.

This is temporary. It will not last forever.

Arash's got you. The pathway of Life's got you. The lifeguard's got you. He's about to throw you that life buoy.

Hold on in that storm.

You are worth it. You're a warrior. You are strong. You're battling the anchor, the trauma, the eye of the hurricane. But rest in the Truth. You're on the verge of pushing that trauma to the bottom of the ocean.

You're about to be the badass war hero. With the ship as your new destination.

God's got you. Lean on him. He can handle your honesty, he can handle your anger, he can handle your frustration and doubt.

*****

You're never closer to God than when you're in the eye of the storm. You're never closer to God than you are when you are suffering. You're never closer to God than when you are on the verge of finally escaping that chain of the anchor.

But remember the path it took to get you here. Following this path of Life is not for the weak. Becoming a ship is not for the weak. Remember what you've been through. Remember this trauma. Remember these fears. & embrace your strength. Embrace what you are capable of. Embrace the journey in front of you.

You don't gain character, grit, perseverance, or authenticity when everything in your life is going perfectly.

Embrace this. You're a warrior in Him now. Be confident. You should be.

& lean on the other fish in the sea. We are battling this crazy storm together!

You may have some of the most fun, most joyful times in your life battling these crazy winds together and finding moments of complete bliss while you dive headfirst into the waves.

I know I did.

Life is just as much beautiful as it is painful.

*****

Chicago Marathon: Mile 25.

Shannon and I are so exhausted that we actually somehow have energy again. The pure adrenaline begins to come flowing back into our veins. This is incomprehensible. We just ran 24 miles, how do we feel more energized during this last mile? That simply doesn't make sense. We are following the song of the ship. We are leaning on each other. We are running solely with our hearts. Our hearts are beating for that ship. I remember why we are running. We are running for Shirley Ryan Ability Lab, where Arash had his physical therapy. I can feel Arash cheering us on from up above. I can feel the higher power in our hearts, in our veins. We cannot finish this race without Him. It's impossible. It's incomprehensible. We are smiling. We are pumped up again. We have adrenaline. We have each other.

Only 1.2 left to go!

*****

A memory resurfaces.

When Arash was sick and I was going to his house every day, I would wake up, I would run, I would eat a healthy breakfast, I would go to Protein Bar and get a smoothie for Arash, and then I would drive to the Perris.

Now that's he not here, I reflect on when I would first ask myself, "Now what?"

I used to blast music the entire time driving to and from the Perris. This was my form of therapy. I would lose myself in the music. I could relate to the pain in the lyrics. Music has never made more sense to me than it did on these drives to the Perris. Music isn't essential. We don't need it for survival. It's a gift. It's a gift from the Ship. It's purely to heal our pain. It's purely to enhance pleasure. It's proof that a higher power exists. A loving, higher power. A power that wants the best for us, despite how it may feel on earth.

I've never enjoyed music more than on those drives to and from the Perris' house.

& even though I'm not driving to the Perris' anymore doesn't mean I can't still enjoy the music.

*****

We are always running for the thrill of it, thrill
    of it
Always pushing up the hill, searching for the
    thrill of it
On and on and on sea are calling out, out again
Never looking down, I'm just in awe of what's in
    front of me

Is it real now?
Two people become one
I can feel it
Two people become one

Thought I'd never see

The love you found in me
Now it's changing all the time
Living in a rhythm where the minute's working
  over time
(Empire of the Sun, "Walking on a Dream")

*****

For a year and a half after Arash died, I truly did not think I would ever recover. I didn't think I would ever be the same. I was surrounded by the demons of trauma, loneliness, pain, suffering, loss, grief. And just when I thought I was about to escape the imprisoning chain of the anchor, the depth of the ocean would just pull me farther down. The demons were everywhere I turned.

The memories of Arash's burial and funeral would keep me up at night, they would awaken me in terror. The casket flooded my vision, the screams echoed in my ears, the smell of death was still lingering in my nostrils.

But I can honestly say they don't anymore.

My relationship has changed with the anchor because my relationship changed with Him.

& I'm realizing that could not have happened without the journey it took to get there.

Yes, there's pain. Yes, there's trauma.

But His beauty, His wonder, His love is greater. Immensely greater.

It's incomprehensible.

It's divine.

I want to live for this pathway now.

I want to live for Life now.

I want to dive headfirst into these currents with no fear, like Arash did.

I want to help other fish swim to the top.

I want to follow that beautiful song playing created by the ship.

*****

Chicago Marathon: Mile 26.

One more to go. It's completely in His Hands.

Shannon turns to me. "We're about to do this, Meg!"

I blacked out during this last mile. But this blackout is the recovery blackout. This is the blackout that I thought I would never recover from while reading Arash's eulogy. Arash is with me in this blackout. He's not in the casket anymore. He's dancing up in the ship. His heart is igniting mine and Shannon's. He's with Shannon and me. We're running for the ship. We're running in perfect rhythm with that Ship's song. For a moment in time, I'm with Arash again. It's the first time we met. I am opening the front door of my Chicago Apartment, and there is his luminous smile. It's contagious, it's infectious. For a moment in time, I'm about to fall in love with him all over again. Everything is completely perfect in this moment.

*****

Teardrops crown the keys on my laptop. I'm in California now. These teardrops are flooding down the streets of California now. But I'm not afraid of the flooding anymore. The flooding in California won't keep me from getting there. These tears are flooding down the hills, down the winding streets, down the edge of Sunset Cliffs into the infinity of the Pacific Ocean. These tears are life giving. These tears are washed into the infinity of the Pacific Ocean the same way Arash's forehead was doused in Holy Water when he first accepted the pathway of Life. When he saw Him.

Chicago Marathon: Mile 26.2.

Last .2 miles to go. We cross the finish line.

Thank you, God.

Thank you for the gift of Arash's love.

& the gift of his suffering.

Thank you for giving us Life.

Thank you.

*****

I feel like we can truly look upward now. Every day, I am making a conscious decision to put that anchor in the past. That anchor is at the bottom of the infinite ocean now. It served its purpose. We learned from it and grew from it, and most importantly, we saw the pathway because of it. For that I am extremely thankful.

I'm thankful for the lifeguard's boss who threw us that lifebuoy and rescued us from the hurricane of the infinite ocean. Now we can sit on the beach in the warm sand and feel safe in this ocean. We can look at this ocean and know that there is a place for us in the ship. There is a seat with our name waiting for us. It's going to take time to get there. We still have many currents to battle to get there. But the strong foundation of the pier at the beach is still there. It's strong. It's stable. It's not going anywhere. It can still weather every storm. It will still stand firm when the ocean waves hit it. It is still holding up the pathway. No matter what. Nothing and nobody can take that pathway away from you.

Remember that.

No current is too harsh. No wave is too big. No challenge is too great. Nobody's perspective or opinion of you can ever take this foundation away. No trauma is greater than this pathway. No fear can compare in the strength of this pathway.

This inspires me, this motivates me.

Life is too beautiful to let the anchor weigh you down.

*****

As I lie on my back in the sand on the shore of Ocean Beach, California, I can't help but notice the lifeguard truck that is driving around the beach. It reminds me of that ambulance that I saw Arash in on my way here. The lifeguards are safe. They're trustworthy. They're cute. They will keep you safe. They have the life buoys on board. They're there if you need them.

I also can't help but notice the airplanes that are flying above me as I gaze into the endless bright blue sky. These planes are flying up above the beach through the sky over the Pacific Ocean. They are roaring loud, but as they move farther away, the roars of their engines are replaced with the soothing sounds of the ocean's waves breaking towards the shore. I watch as these airplanes fade into the infinity of the sky. They begin to get smaller and smaller in my vision, and finally they're gone. Out of sight. They're traveling through the infinity of the sky over the infinity of the ocean, & in this moment, I'm completely conscious of God's presence yet again. Our loved ones are on those planes. They may have already become ships and escaped the ocean that we're still currently in. But they're safe. Now, they've transformed to planes. They're safe. They're watching over us. They're on their way to their next adventure.

We'll see them again.

*****

Our loved ones' bodies may be in caskets in the bottom of the ocean, but their spirits, their souls are in these airplanes up above us. Protecting us, watching us, guiding us.

He already purchased that airplane ticket for us. So I'm going to be patient until it's time to take flight. & enjoy the journey.

About the Author